THE HARMONY OF THE
PROPHETIC WORD

THE HARMONY

OF THE

PROPHETIC WORD

A KEY TO OLD TESTAMENT PROPHECY
CONCERNING THINGS TO COME

BY

ARNO C. GAEBELEIN

Editor of "Our Hope." Author of "Exposition of Matthew,"
"Studies in Zechariah," "The Jewish Question,"
"Annotated Bible" (9 vols.),
"Half a Century," etc.

Publication Office, "Our Hope"

456 Fourth Avenue

New York City

CONTENTS

FOREWORD

HAVING had the privilege of reading advance sheets of the present book, it is both a pleasure and a privilege to commend it to all who are interested in the study of "the prophetic Word made surer" (2 Peter 1: 19). All students of prophecy are sure to be interested in a presentation of the chief con-tents of the prophetic Scriptures which is so original in scope and method.

But I would more especially bespeak for this book the attention of those who are *not* students of prophecy. Unfortunately this class includes the enormous majority of present-day believers. No fact is at once more patent or more lamentable than that the writings of the prophets are little read and less comprehended.

Doubtless there are many reasons for this condi-tion. The characteristic of the present age is a reckless and unreasoning optimism. On every hand we are assured that the church is " marching grandly on to the conquest of the world," and that despite the fact that after one hundred years of missions there are 200,000,000 more heathen to convert than at the beginning of that century. But prophecy, grandly optimistic in its ultimate view, presents any-thing but a flattering picture of the end of this age,

Apostasy, heading up in the man of sin, and the utter destruction of the present imposing world-system by a crushing blow, is the testimony of the prophets. This is an unwelcome message, and therefore is not heeded. It is pleasanter to listen to the self-sent prophets who prophesy "smooth things."

Another reason for the neglect of prophecy is found in the undeniable difficulties which encounter the beginner in that study. A bewildering number of new phrases and formulæ are encountered, and it is not all at once, nor indeed without long application, that this seeming confusion falls into its truly majestic order.

It is precisely at this point that "The Harmony of the Prophetic Word" seems to me supremely helpful. What the beginner could not do at all, nor even the most persevering student for many months, is here done for him by an expert student of the prophetic writings.

The *method,* as will be seen by an examination of the book, is to take up the great prophetic epochs and events, and bring together from the whole body of prophecy the testimony concerning them. This, indeed, thoroughly as the author has done his work, will not be found available as a substitute for personal study of these great subjects—nor was such substitution any part of the thought of the author —but what the present book does do is to present the great subjects concerning which God has re-

FOREWORD

vealed the future, and so to assemble and analyse that revelation that any reader of the book will find himself fully introduced to these great and important themes.

The final effect of such a synthesis is to leave the mind overwhelmingly impressed with the divine origin and authorship of these ancient oracles. Writing in widely separated ages, under wholly different circumstances, of necessity often ignorant of each other's writings, the production of one continuous, harmoniously developed testimony is proof unanswerable that, though He employed many penmen, God alone is the Author of the prophetic testimony.

C. I. SCOFIELD.

EAST NORTHFIELD, MASS.

1

INTRODUCTORY

THE harmony which exists throughout the Bible, from Genesis to Revelation, is one of the strongest arguments for the plenary inspiration of the Scriptures. The unity which we find here is supernatural; it is divine. The inspired writers of the Bible cover a period of almost two thousand years, living in so many different ages and under different circumstances, yet all agree perfectly, and there is no clash of opinions. Such unity is a miracle. No human genius could produce it. There is nothing like it in all the literary products of men, and there will be nothing like it in the future. *God* spake at sundry times and in divers manners (Heb. 1: 1), and therefore all in this precious Book being God-breathed (2 Tim. 3:16), must be a perfect, infallible whole. What an awful sin to criticise the Bible, to deny its inspiration, to put the Word of God which He has exalted above all His Name upon the same level with profane literature. Yet this is the common drift of our times.

Because the Bible *is* the Word of God and the same Spirit of God spoke in and through the different instruments, therefore its Divine unity. This unity is not confined to matters pertaining to salvation, but it also exists throughout the prophetic Word. Indeed, we shall see that nowhere is the Divine unity of the Scriptures so evident as in Prophecy.

In the first and second Epistles of Peter we find two passages which speak of the importance and the content of the prophetic Word. These two Epistles are certainly the right place for such statements, for they are addressed to the sojourners in the dispersion, and believers are viewed in them as pilgrims and strangers.

We turn first to the second Epistle of Peter:

"And we have the prophetic Word made surer, to which ye do well taking heed, as to a lamp shining in a dark place until the day dawn and the morning star arise in your hearts: Knowing this first, that the scope of no prophecy of Scripture is had from its own particular interpretation, for prophecy was not ever uttered by the will of man, but holy men of God spake under the power of the Holy Spirit." (2 Pet. 1 : 19-21.)

We remember that Peter mentions in the first chapter of his second Epistle the transfiguration of our Lord, and speaks of it as manifesting the power and coming of our Lord Jesus Christ. That scene on the holy mountain of which he had been eyewitness was a foreshadowing of the return of the Lord, visibly and gloriously, to the earth. The entire Old Testament prophecy speaks of this great event, the visible coming and manifestation of Jehovah, therefore the transfiguration of our Lord is a confirmation of Old Testament prophetic predictions, and more than that, the earnest of their final and complete fulfilment. In this sense we have the prophetic Word as found in the Old Testament made surer, for in the transfiguration we see precisely that which prophet after prophet had declared. In the above passage we also read the comparison which is made between the prophetic Word and a lamp, and we are exhorted to take heed to it. This God-given lamp shone out from the beginning. Its light was kindled by Jehovah in the garden, its first ray fell upon the guilty pair and brought them hope and cheer, as well as guidance through the dark night outside of Eden. It continued its blessed shining; new oil was constantly added to it. By its light generation after generation by *taking heed to it* found joy and comfort as faith looked on towards the future. And this lamp, the prophetic Word, is still shining, and we are, like all believers before us, to take heed to it. The " dark place " is the present age, still an evil age. But the lamp will not shine for ever. When the morning comes we blow out our lamps; they are needed no longer. The day will dawn, the Sun of Righteousness will rise, and then the lamp will shine no more, for what the mouth of all His holy prophets declared, the blessed Kingdom has come. Before the day dawn comes the rising of the Morning star, which is Christ Himself, coming for His saints. This precedes the day dawn.

Furthermore, notice this passage teaches that no prophecy explains itself as such, none stands for itself. God's purposes are revealed in it progressively from beginning to end. Holy men of God spake, and each of them and all of them were moved by the same Spirit; therefore the entire prophetic Word *must* be harmonious, and it must be studied as a whole, comparing Scripture with Scripture.

Another striking passage is found in the first Epistle of Peter:

"Concerning which salvation prophets who have prophesied of the grace towards you sought out and searched out; searching what, or what manner of time the Spirit of Christ which was in them pointed out, testifying before of the sufferings which belonged to Christ, and the glories after these. To whom it was revealed, that not to themselves but to you they ministered those things, which have now been announced to you by those who have declared to you the glad tidings by the Holy Spirit sent from heaven, which angels desire to look into." (1 Pet. 1: 10-13.)

The prophets were visited by the Spirit of Christ, and He prophesied through them. After they had written down their prophecies they began to read them, and were not able to understand them fully. Not one of the Old Testament prophets had the knowledge of God's purposes and the things to come which we as believers in Christ may have, for we *have* the Holy Spirit dwelling in us. But the main thought in these words is the content of the entire prophetic Word. The Spirit of *Christ*

14

in them pointed out and testified before of the *sufferings* which belonged to Christ, and the *glories* after these.

This makes it very clear that the prophetic Word contains two great sections—the sufferings and the glories, and the centre, Christ. The person of Christ, His sufferings in humiliation, the glories which are His in the future exaltation are the great themes of Old Testament prophecy. How truly He said Himself concerning the Scriptures, " They testify of Me " (John 5: 30). They testify of the cross and the crown, the first coming and the second coming, the humiliation and the exaltation.

It is not our intention to trace the prophecies which relate to the sufferings. This has often been done before. They are past, Christ suffered once. They were minutely foretold. The whole path of the Messiah from His birth in Bethlehem to the sufferings on the cross, His humiliation and rejection, was made known through the prophets; all these predictions have found in our Lord their *literal* fulfilment. The literal fulfilment of prophecies relating to the humiliation of the Christ is a warrant for the literal fulfilment of the prophecies relating to the glories of the same Lord and Christ. How inconsequent are many interpreters of the prophetic Word in their defence of the literal fulfilment of the sufferings of Christ and the spiritualizing of the prophecies which speak of the glories to come. The sufferings were literal, the glories are literal also. The New Testament gives no reason whatever for the spiritualizing of the Old Testament predictions of the coming glories. It indorses the literal fulfilment of unfilled Old Testament prophecy.

II

THE DAY OF JEHOVAH

OUR first aim will be to show that the entire prophetic Word predicts a day and a time when Jehovah will be revealed in the earth. This day is called repeatedly the day of Jehovah, a day of wrath and of judgment. A day followed by a continued manifestation of the Glory of the Lord and His righteous rule, as well as great blessings for the earth and its inhabitants. It has not yet come, and is still future. How prophecy harmonizes in speaking of this great future day we will now demonstrate. We have a continued and a progressive revelation of it which is not confined to the Old Testament prophets, but extends to the New Testament, with a fitting climax in the last book, the Revelation of Jesus Christ.

We do not begin with the prophet Isaiah, whose book is generally considered to be the first prophetic book of the Old Testament. Old Testament prophecy is not contained exclusively in the books which are called " Prophets." Moses and David as well as other men were prophets. Most of the songs in the Bible are not only hymns of praise, but they breathe a prophetic spirit.

In the 23d and 24th chapters of the book of Numbers we find recorded a series of utterances by the Spirit of God through one who had been called by an enemy to curse God's people. Balaam had to speak and pronounce the blessing, and could not help it. His parables do not alone declare the blessedness of God's earthly people Israel, with many precious applications to the believer in Christ, but they also unfold what shall be in the end.

In Numbers 24: 17 we have a statement from the lips of this seer to which we call special attention:

"I shall see Him, but not now. I shall behold Him, but not nigh. There cometh a Star out of Jacob, and a Sceptre shall rise out of Israel, and He shall cut in pieces the corners of Moab and destroy all the sons of tumult."

Reading on to the end of the chapter we find that the Spirit of God through Balaam predicts that when the Sceptre, rising out of Israel, has full sway, the nations will be punished. The quoted verse has always been interpreted by orthodox Jewish, as well as by most Christian, commentators as referring to the Messiah. We have in it His first coming, "A Star out of Jacob," His second coming, "A Sceptre out of Israel." When He arises as a Sceptre assuming the rule, it will be to destroy the sons of tumult and to consume His enemies. The Star has shone forth. The Sceptre will arise by and by.

In the 32d chapter of Deuteronomy we find

another great prophecy. Moses sings here his wonderful prophetic song. What he utters as a farewell to his beloved people is a grand outline of their future history, their apostasy, their subsequent deliverance and restoration to their own land. It is a marvellous prediction, an unanswerable argument in itself for the Divinity of the Bible. It is " a key to all prophecy." * At the close of this song, before the announcement that nations shall in future rejoice with His people (verse 43), we read of what Jehovah will do:

> "If I have sharpened my gleaming sword,
>   And my hand take hold of judgment,
> I will render vengeance to mine adversaries,
>   And will recompense them that hate me.
> Mine arrows will I make drunk with blood,
>   And my sword shall devour flesh."
>
> (Verses 41 and 42.)

Some expositors have admired the language of these stanzas, but have entirely ignored their prophetic meaning. They reveal a time of future judgment.

The nations do not yet rejoice with God's earthly people Israel, the divine sword of retribution has not yet been unsheathed, and the day of vengeance is still future. The One of whom Moses speaks as coming to take hold of *judgment* is the " Sceptre out of Israel " of Balaam's parable. It is He who in His humiliation said to His enemies, " Before

* Professor Franz Delitsch.

19

Abraham was *I am,"* Jehovah-Jesus. The words in Moses' song, quoted above, predict His coming as Judge in that day.

We listen next to the language of a mother in Israel. Hannah sings a song—praising Jehovah for mercies received. Her song is not less prophetic than Moses' sublime prophecy. In 1 Sam. 2:10 we read at the end of Hannah's song:

> "They that strive with Jehovah shall be broken to pieces;
> In the heavens will He thunder upon them.
> Jehovah will judge the ends of the earth;
> And He will give strength unto His King,
> And exalt the horn of His anointed."

These words, equally sublime, predict a future judgment, a time in which the ends of the earth will be dealt with by the Lord, when the Messiah will be exalted. Here then we have three persons as different as they can be—Balaam, the unwilling prophet; Moses, the great leader of God's people; and Hannah, a mother in Israel. All are moved by the same Spirit, who makes them His mouthpiece, and each declares that Jehovah will judge the nations and the earth. What a striking harmony we have in this!

Hannah's song is but a faint beginning of what the Holy Spirit unfolds in inspired song in perfect, Divine order in that wonderful collection of songs, *the Book of Psalms.* We generally look upon the Psalms as expressing all kinds of human experiences, and we often draw much comfort from them.

That we can do this none would dispute. However, if we wish to know the full meaning of this book, we must look upon it as a *prophetic* book.

It is a well-known fact that the Psalms are divided into five books. These five books correspond to the five books of Moses or the Pentateuch. So clear is the correspondency that the old rabbis called the Psalms the Pentateuch of David.

The *Genesis* portion of the Psalms extends from Psalm 1 to 41. Many of the Messianic Psalms are found in this section. Its character is like Genesis. It begins with " Blessed is the man " (Psalm 1), which is the Lord Jesus Christ, and it ends with " Blessed is he that considereth the poor," and this is the same Lord. The whole section ends with " Blessed be the Lord God of Israel from everlasting and to everlasting " (Psalm 41 : 13).

The *Exodus* part begins with Psalm 42 and ends with Psalm 72. Like in the book of Exodus do we find here the suffering of Israel's remnant and how they are delivered. This section is rich in dispensational foreshadowings of Israel's future. It begins with the cry for the tabernacle and ends with the vision of the kingdom established. " He shall judge the poor of the people, He shall save the children of the needy, and shall break in pieces the oppressor." " He shall have dominion also from sea to sea, and from the river unto the ends of the earth " (Psl. 72 : 8). This section ends with a fuller praise

than the first. " Blessed be the Lord God, the God
of Israel, who only doeth wondrous things. And
blessed be His glorious name for ever; and let the
whole earth be filled with His glory; Amen and
Amen " (Psl. 72 : 18, 19).

The *third* book begins with Psalm 73 and closes
with 89. The very beginning of this part makes it a
Leviticus. The opening Psalms are the gift of the
Spirit through Asaph, and they celebrate the holiness of God. " Truly God is good to Israel, to
such that are of a clean heart " (Psl. 73 : 1). This
refers us to the remnant of Israel in the last days.
The last Psalm in this section rehearses God's wonderful doings in behalf of His people and puts before us the sure mercies of David, that is the full rati-
fication of the Davidic covenant, and how One from
David is to be exalted. " And I will make Him my
firstborn, higher than the kings of the earth " (Psl.
89 : 27). The ending is, " Blessed be the Lord for-
evermore. Amen and Amen."

The *fourth* part or book extends from Psalm 90
to Psalm 106. This is in character like the book of
Numbers. Here we see Israel in the wilderness; all
her ways are traced, but Israel is seen in this section led out of that wilderness and come into her
inheritance. The opening Psalm, the 90th, is significant. It is the only Psalm we have, given by
Moses, the leader of the people. It speaks of death,
and is rightly called the Psalm of the old creation;
the 91st is the Psalm of the new creation. While

in the 90th we see the first man, in the 91st we behold the second man. This is the shortest section. In the 103d Israel, redeemed from all her backslidings, sings her new song: "Bless the Lord, O my soul; and all that is within me, bless His holy name. Bless the Lord, O my soul, and forget not all His benefits. Who forgiveth all thine iniquities; who healeth all thy diseases; who redeemeth thy life from destruction; who crowneth thee with loving kindness and tender mercies." Then comes the 104th, the praise of nature. The 105th and 106th are the praise of His restored people, and the doxology in the last verse of the 106th contains the nation's praise: "Blessed be the Lord God of Israel from everlasting to everlasting, and let all the people say, Amen. Praise ye the Lord."

Still more interesting is the *fifth* or Deuteronomy part, the last book in the Psalms. Like Deuteronomy, it puts before us the end of the ways of God with His people. This section begins with the 107th and leads to the close of the book.

The opening is highly instructive. "O give thanks unto the Lord, for He is good; for His mercy endureth for ever. Let the redeemed of the Lord say so, whom He hath redeemed from the hand of the enemy, and gathered them out of the lands, from the East and from the West, from the North and from the South." Deuteronomy shows us, in its closing chapters, how Israel is to be scattered into the corners of the earth. All this has been and is being fulfilled. But there is also the promise that they should be gathered again: " . . . Then the Lord thy God will turn thy captivity, and have compassion upon thee, and will return and gather thee from all the nations whither the Lord thy God hath scattered thee" (Deut. 30: 3). Here in the 107th Psalm we find the fulfilment of this prophecy. This section, and with it the whole book, ends in a continued "Hallelujah." Praise ye the Lord. All is praising Jehovah. Israel, redeemed, praises Him, the nations, all creation, everything that has breath, praise Him. Here we have the great end of all things, the praise and worship of God.

Throughout the Psalms we read of Jehovah's intervention in behalf of His suffering earthly people, His manifestation in glory and wrath upon His enemies. To say that these events were fulfilled in David's experience, or find now a spiritual fulfilment in the church, is doing great violence to the Scriptures. It dishonours God and His Word. Beginning with the 2d Psalm, where the coming King is seen enthroned upon the holy hill of Zion, ruling the nations with a rod of iron and smashing them like potters' vessels, we can trace the day of Jehovah's manifestation through the entire book, and hear again and again of the overthrow of God's enemies, the deliverance of His people, and the establishment of His rule. A closer study of the Psalms and a literal interpretation of all they declare will make this clear to the reader. Here in-

deed is a mine of wealth in prophetic foreshadowings which is inexhaustible.

The phrase, " Day of Jehovah," and its fuller
revelation we find only in the books which
are generally called the Prophets. " In that day,"
is a phrase which occurs many times in those prophetic books. *Obadiah* and *Joel* are the earliest
of prophets. In the fifteenth verse of Obadiah we
read :

"For the day of Jehovah is near upon all the nations;
as thou hast done, it shall be done unto thee; thy recompense shall return upon thine own head."

This prophet ends after a description of the day
of Jehovah with the declaration, " the kingdom
shall be the Lord's."

It is, however, in *Joel* (Jehovah is God) that we
find full mention of Jehovah's day. He may well
be called the prophet of the day of Jehovah. This
day is the burden of his prophecy. It is also evident that there is between this early prophet and
the prophets which followed the closest relation.
Higher criticism declares that the other prophets took
the wonderful flow of language and the visions of
Joel as a pattern and attempted to imitate it; while
others maintain that Joel lived after the exile and
copied in his terse style from the writings of the
other prophets which preceded him. The Spirit of
God unfolds in the later prophets what He had
given in Joel, so to speak, in a nutshell. No prophet

" imitated " another; each wrote as moved by the Holy Spirit.

In Joel we read five times of the day of Jehovah. Swarms of locusts had fallen into the land of Israel. Behind this great calamity there looms up a greater one. The swarms of locusts are but types of enemies who are to fall into the land, and in the midst of all the dreadful scenes of famine and desolation the prophet points to the day of Jehovah and describes that solemn day. See chapters 1:15; 2: 1-2, 10-11, 30-31; in the 3d chapter this great day is vividly portrayed:

"The day of Jehovah is at hand in the valley of decision. The sun and the moon shall be darkened, and the stars shall withdraw their shining. And Jehovah shall roar out of Zion, and utter His voice from Jerusalem, and the heavens and the earth shall shake" (3: 15, 16).

Turning to *Amos,* the herdsman of Tekoa, we find the day mentioned in the very beginning, chapter 1:2. Here Jehovah roars from Zion against the ungodly nations. While the judgment of the nations, as announced through Amos, has seen a partial fulfilment in the judgments of these nations which are mentioned, its final great fulfilment is yet to come. The day of the Lord will bring this.

The testimony of the prophet *Hosea* is mostly about the rejection of Israel and Judah and their final restoration and blessedness as a nation, and one would not expect the announcement of that day in this prophet. However, it is clearly indicated in the 11th chapter:

"I will not execute the fierceness of My anger;
I will not again destroy Ephraim:
For I am God and not man:
In the midst of thee is the Holy One,
And I will not come in wrath (to His earthly people).
They shall walk after Jehovah.
He shall roar like a lion;
When He shall roar (in that day), then the children shall
    hasten from the West,
They shall hasten as a bird out of Egypt
And as a dove out of Assyria,
And I will cause them to dwell in their houses, saith Jeho-
    vah."   (Chapter 11:9-11.)

In the vision of Isaiah, which so vividly shows the suffering and exaltation of the Servant of Jehovah, the Messiah, as well as the glorious future of Israel, the day of the Lord is often mentioned. Throughout this prophet this day is seen in a threefold relation. The day brings the visible, glorious manifestation of Jehovah. It also brings the deliverance and restoration of the remnant of His earthly people and the overthrow and judgment of their enemies.

In the beginning of Isaiah there stands a sublime description of that day, the day when Jehovah arises and man's day is ended:

"For there shall be a day of Jehovah of hosts upon everything proud and lofty, and upon everything lifted up, and it shall be brought low; and upon all the cedars of Lebanon, high and lifted up, and upon all the oaks of

Bashan; and upon all the lofty mountains, and upon all the hills that are lifted up; and upon every high tower, and upon every fenced wall; and upon all the ships of Tarshish, and upon all pleasant works of art. And the loftiness of men shall be brought low; and Jehovah alone shall be exalted in that day: and the idols shall utterly pass away. And they shall go into the caves of the rocks, and into the holes of the earth, from before the terror of Jehovah, and from the glory of His majesty, when He shall arise to terrify the earth. In that day men shall cast away their idols of silver and their idols of gold, which they made each for himself to worship, to the moles and to the bats; to go into the clefts of the rocks and into the fissures of the cliffs, from before the terror of Jehovah, and from the glory of His majesty, when He shall arise to terrify the earth" (Isa. 2:12-21).

This and similar passages in the opening chapters of Isaiah point clearly to the great day of Jehovah, and it is seen at once that the vision of Isaiah concerning that day is in harmony with what we have learned so far from the other Scriptures.

The 4th chapter in Isaiah unfolds the blessed results following the terrible day of the Lord, which, in its fury, is announced in the 2d and 3d chapters. Chapter 10:5-34, contains a description of the events connected with the approaching day, events which will transpire in Israel's land, while in the 11th chapter, beginning with the fourth verse, still greater blessings are announced to follow the appearing of Him who " shall smite the earth with the rod of His mouth, and with the breath of His lips slay the wicked." No intelligent believer could claim that these scenes, as predicted in Isaiah 11, are now seen in the earth; for the spiritualizing of them we have no authority.

Another prediction is recorded in the 13th chapter, the chapter which begins a new section in that prophet, announcing the judgment of nations, partly fulfilled, yet finally to be fulfilled in Jehovah's day. We quote from this chapter:

"Behold, the day of Jehovah cometh, cruel both with wrath and fierce anger, to lay the earth desolate; and He will destroy the sinners thereof out of it. For the stars of the heavens and the constellations thereof shall not give their light; the sun shall be darkened in his going forth, and the moon shall not cause her light to shine. And I will punish the world for evil, and the wicked for their iniquity; and I will make the arrogance of the proud to cease, and will bring low the haughtiness of the violent. I will make a man more precious than fine gold, even man than the gold of Ophir. Therefore I will make the heavens to shake, and the earth shall be removed out of her place, at the wrath of Jehovah of hosts, and in the day of His fierce anger" (Isa. 13:9-13).

Beginning with chapter 24, and ending with the 27th chapter, we find a vision which has justly been called "Isaiah's Apocalypse." Here we have a continuation of the description of the day of the Lord. The wrath of the Lord is again announced. The earth is seen emptied, utterly broken down, dissolved, violently moved, reeling to and fro like a drunkard, and shaken like a night hut (chapter 24: 18-20). Alongside of the wrath we have the glorious singing of a delivered people, the assurance of the binding of the enemy, the resurrection of the dead, the conversion of the nations. All this is closely connected in Isaiah, 24th and 27th, with the day of Jehovah.

The 40th chapter, that chapter of comfort for Jerusalem, is not silent about Jehovah's manifestation, for Jerusalem's comfort begins with the manifestation of the Lord. " Every valley shall be raised up, and every mountain and hill shall be brought low; and the crooked shall be made straight, and the rough places a plain. And the glory of Jehovah shall be revealed, and all flesh shall see it together, for the mouth of Jehovah hath spoken" (Is. 40: 4, 5).

Some of the other passages in Isaiah speaking of the Lord's day and His manifestation are the following: 61: 2; 63: 1-6; 66: 6, 15, 16, 23, and 24.

When we turn to the prophet *Jeremiah,* we discover that the Spirit of God announces through him likewise such a day as He did through the other men of God. We quote two passages:

"And thou, prophesy unto them all these words, and say unto them, Jehovah will roar from on high, and utter His voice from His holy habitation, He will mightily roar upon His dwelling place, He will give a shout, as they that tread the vintage, against all the inhabitants of the earth. The noise shall come to the end of the earth; for Jehovah has a controversy with the nations, He entereth into judgment with all flesh; as for the wicked, He will give them up to the sword, saith Jehovah. Thus saith Jehovah of hosts: Behold evil shall go forth from nation to nation, and a great storm shall be raised up from the uttermost parts of the earth. And the slain of Jehovah shall be at that day

from one end of the earth even unto the other end of the
earth; they shall not be lamented, neither gathered nor
buried; they shall be dung upon the face of the ground"
(Jer. 25:30-33).

We learn from this prediction what we have
learned before from others: the day is coming for
the entire earth, and evil will go from nation to
nation.

The second passage we quote is from chapter
30:18-24:

"Behold a tempest of Jehovah, fury is gone forth, a
sweeping storm; it shall whirl down upon the head of the
wicked. The fierce anger of Jehovah shall not return, until
He have executed, and until He have performed the purpose
of His heart. At the end of the days ye shall consider."

The "end of the days" has not yet been reached.
It is still future. After God's purpose in this present age, the gathering out from the nations a people
for His name, is accomplished, then shall He perform the purpose of His heart.

Read also Jeremiah 4:23-26.

The prophet *Ezekiel* is but little studied as a
book. Like every other book in the Bible, it has
perfect order. It is divided into three parts. The
first part, chapters 1-24; the second part, chapters
25-32; and the third part, from chapter 33 to the
end.

The first twenty-four chapters contain prophecies
which were delivered by him before the destruction

of Jerusalem. The sins of Judah and Samaria are vividly described and the threatening judgments announced. The sins enumerated are idolatry, adultery, fornication, usury, bloodshed, oppression, and theft. Beginning with the description of the likeness of the glory of the Lord, a glory which is yet to be manifested, for the whole earth to see, every chapter burns with holy zeal for God and overflows with wonderful descriptions of human failure and sin, divine forbearance, righteousness, and the coming day of the vengeance of God.

The 16th chapter is one of the finest in the first part of the book. The 24th chapter begins with the parable of the boiling pot, typical of Jerusalem's judgment; but the chapter ends with a promise for the escaped, not only applicable to the escaped then, but also to the remnant of Israel in a future day.

The second part contains the announcement of the judgment of seven nations and cities. These are: Ammon, Moab, Edom, Philistia, Tyre, Zidon, and Egypt. These prophecies were given after the destruction of Jerusalem. The judgments upon these nations are prophecies of the judgment of nations in *the day of the Lord*. The great nations now in existence may read their coming doom here as nations. Read chapters 27, 28, and compare them with Revelation 18. Yet while Israel's enemies are destroyed and their destruction is announced, Israel's Hope shines bright upon the dark background of divine judgment.

While the term " day of the Lord " is not mentioned in the prophet *Daniel,* this great event is nevertheless clearly revealed throughout the great prophecies of Daniel. The great image which Nebuchadnezzar saw in his dream, presents, according to divine interpretation, the four great world powers. The stone, cut out without hands, falling down and striking the image at its toes, pulverizing it, while the stone becomes a great mountain filling the entire earth, is the day of the Lord. Gentile world rule will not cease till He comes. Our Lord speaks of this demolishing of the rule of ungodly nations when He said: " And whosoever shall fall on this stone shall be broken: *but on whomsoever it shall fall, it will grind him to powder* " (Matt. 21: 44).

In the 7th chapter Daniel sees in his vision again the day of the Lord, and Him, Jehovah, as Son of Man coming in the clouds of heaven. All the other events which cluster around the day of Jehovah are also predicted in Daniel.

In the prophet *Micah,* at the close of that beautiful fifth chapter, where the Lord's first and second coming is so clearly described, we read: " And I will execute vengeance in anger and in fury upon the nations, such as they have not heard of " (5: 15). The context shows this will be in connection with God's earthly people in their final restoration.

Nahum prophesied against Nineveh, the wicked

city, her wickedness come to the full. That ancient,
bloody city, in its awful overthrow, is the prophetic
picture of the great and wicked city of the end, and
a prediction of the final overthrow of all which is
wicked in the earth. Read Nahum, 1 : 1-9, and see
how it harmonises with all the rest. *Habakkuk* in
his vision beholds the Lord's coming in vengeance
for the judgment of the nations and the salvation of
His people (chapter 3). *Zephaniah* may also, like
Joel, be termed "the prophet of the day of the
Lord." Like Joel's three chapters, the three of
Zephaniah witness fully to that coming dreadful
day, and the blessings which are in store for Israel.

Perhaps in the 1st chapter of Zephaniah (Jehovah hides) we have the finest description of the
day:

"The great day of Jehovah is near;
  It is near and hasteneth greatly.
  The voice of the day of Jehovah.
  The mighty man shall cry there bitterly.
  A day of wrath is that day,
  A day of trouble and distress,
  A day of ruin and desolation,
  A day of darkness and gloom,
  A day of clouds and gross darkness,
  A day of the trumpet and alarm
  Against the fenced cities
  And against the high battlements.
  And I will bring distress upon men,
  And they shall walk like blind men;
  For they have sinned against Jehovah;
  Their blood shall be poured out like dust
  And their flesh like dung.

Their silver and their gold shall not be able to deliver them
In the day of Jehovah's wrath;
And the whole land shall be devoured by the fire of His
jealousy,
For He will make an end,
Yea, a sudden one, shall He make of all them that dwell
in the land" (Zeph. 1:14-18).

It is clearly seen what wonderful agreement there
is between this utterance and those of Isaiah, Joel,
Habakkuk, and the other prophets. Other passages
in Zephaniah which speak of the day of Jehovah
are the following: Chapters 2:1-3, 8-15; 3:11,
16, etc.

Haggai sees the day: "For thus saith the Lord
of hosts: Yet once it is a little while, and I will
shake the heavens and the earth, and the sea and
the dry land. And I will shake all nations, and the
desire of all nations shall come; and I will fill this
house with glory, saith the Lord of Hosts" (2:
6, 7). This is still future (compare with Heb.
12:26-29). *Zechariah's* night visions* are likewise in part descriptive of events connected with
that day, such as the punishment of the nations, the
regathering of Israel, the establishment of the theocratic rule, and future glory in the earth. The last
chapter is taken up with a detailed account of the
events of that day.

In that chapter Jehovah's visible manifestation to
fight against the nations that have come against

* *Studies in Zechariah,* by A. C. Gaebelein, gives a complete
analysis and exposition of this interesting book.

Jerusalem is foretold; and what follows in this chapter of the prophet whose name means " Jehovah remembers " may be termed a fitting climax of Old Testament prophecy concerning the great coming day of Jehovah.

But *Malachi,* the last book of the Old Testament, is likewise not silent on the day of Jehovah:

"For behold, the day cometh, burning as a furnace; and all the proud and all that work wickedness shall be stubble; and the day that cometh shall burn them up, saith Jehovah of hosts, so that it shall leave them neither root nor branch " (4: 1).

And this word, which harmonizes so fully with all we have learned before, is followed by the gracious announcement to God's earthly people:

"And unto you that fear my name shall the Sun of Righteousness arise with healing in his wings; and ye shall go forth and leap like fatted calves. And ye shall tread down the wicked; for they shall be ashes under the soles of your feet in the day that I prepare, saith Jehovah of hosts." (Mal. 4: 2, 3.)

We have thus briefly shown that Old Testament prophecy harmonizes completely in the prediction of the great day of Jehovah. We have seen how various, yet harmonious, the prophecies are which relate to this day. If they are thus put together, what a solemn picture they unfold before our eyes! Unbelief may laugh at it and ridicule him who expects a fulfilment of these majestic scenes of Jehovah's manifestation. A false interpretation of God's Word, in the end nothing less than unbelief, may spiritualize these predictions and call them fulfilled in past events; but the believer, who knows God means what He says, reads these revelations in faith and enters into the thoughts and purposes of God. Faith sees them as being literally fulfilled and rejoices in the assurance of deliverance from the day of the darkening sun and the fierce wrath of God.

We wish to add that this day of the Lord must not be looked upon as a day of twenty-four hours. It is more or less descriptive of the entire age which is to come; it will last a thousand years. "For a thousand years in Thy sight are but as yesterday, when it is past" (Ps. 90:4.). "One day is with the Lord as a thousand years, and a thousand years as one day" (2 Pet. 3:8.). Now it is still *man's* day, and it has lasted thousands of years. The same as the hour which our Lord mentions in John 5:25, when the dead should hear His voice, means this age, and that hour is not yet past. So, when the Lord comes and is manifested in His glory, the day of man ends and the Lord's day begins. The glorious manifestation of Jehovah-Jesus, and His righteous judgment, will last for a thousand years (Rev. 20:4).

And now but a rapid glance at the New Testament. Are the New Testament Scriptures silent as to this great day, that day of fire and wrath, the day of the nations' calamity and upheaval, of a visible manifestation of Jehovah's glory and the establishment of His rule? They are not; but make known this day in fullest harmony with the Scriptures contained in the Old Testament.

John the Baptist appears, and in harmony with the Old Testament, to which he belongs, announces the first and second coming of Christ. He speaks of the *fire* baptism which He brings. This is not a spiritual experience of the believer, but the second coming of Christ. "Whose fan is in His hand, and He will thoroughly purge His floor, and gather His wheat into the garner; but He will burn up the chaff with unquenchable fire." (Matt. 3: 12.)

Then our Lord referred many times while in the earth to that day of His own glory. Whenever He speaks of His coming as *Son of Man* it refers to His visible manifestations from Heaven in His own day. Nowhere is His coming for His saints, when He comes in the air (1 Thess. 4: 13-18), described as a coming of the *Son of Man,* but as Lord. In Matt. 24: 29, 30, our Lord gives a full description of His glorious coming as Son of Man. It does hardly need any further word of comment to show how closely these two verses are linked with the descriptions of Jehovah's appearing in the prophets. Daniel, Isaiah, Joel, Habakkuk, Zephaniah, Zechariah, etc., gave utterance through the Spirit of Christ concerning "His Glories," and in Matthew the Lord Himself, whose Spirit revealed all this to the prophets, presses it all together in a few sentences, and in the presence of His disciples He witnesses of His own glory to come at the end of the age. He speaks of Himself in Matt. 25:31, as sitting upon the throne of His glory to judge the nations.

Of the many passages to which we could refer we take but a few. In 1 Thessalonians we have alongside of the blessed hope of the Lord's coming for His saints, mention made of the *day of the Lord*. It is in the 5th chapter (1 Thess, 5:2). It is clearly seen that day does not concern believers in Christ. The day cometh with sudden destruction upon the careless and ungodly world. In the 1st chapter of the Second Epistle we read of this day again in the following words:

"When the Lord Jesus shall be revealed from Heaven with His mighty angels. In flaming fire taking vengeance on them that know not God, and that obey not the Gospel of our Lord Jesus Christ; who shall be punished with everlasting destruction from the presence of the Lord and from the glory of His power" (2 Thess. 1:7-9.)

In 2 Peter, 3:10, we find likewise a description of the day of the Lord:

"But the day of the Lord will come as a thief in the night; in the which the heavens shall pass away with a great noise, and the elements shall melt with fervent heat, the earth also and the works that are therein shall be burned up."

This passage has brought a difficulty to many believers. Post-millennialism, which teaches that the Millennium, the thousand years of peace on earth

and glory to God in the highest, will come before
the Lord comes, and that the Second Advent in the
day of the Lord brings the burning up of the earth,
has used this passage as a strong argument. The
apparent difficulty vanishes when we look upon the
day of the Lord as the age to come, being a thousand years. That day, lasting a thousand years,
will have a beginning with fire, and after the thousand years there will be an end with fire. In 2
Peter the beginning as well as the end of that long
day is before us.

The book of Revelation is, after the 5th chapter, full of descriptions of events which we find predicted by the prophets and in the Psalms, and all
relate to the day of Jehovah. In Isaiah we found
the prediction of men hiding themselves in the caves
and the rocks for fear of the Lord, and in the Revelation we read similar words (6: 12-17). We have
also the darkened sun and moon, the trembling
earth, the falling stars, the shaking of the heavens,
in this last book of the Bible, which we find in the
rest of the prophetic Word. The climax of all is the
opened heavens and the manifestation of Jehovah
at the head of the armies of Heaven (Rev. 19).

May our hearts as believers praise Him who has
redeemed us by His blood and delivered us from
the wrath to come. Blessedly and forever true it
is, he that believeth in Him hath everlasting life and
shall not come into judgment. (John 5: 24.)

III

THE GREAT TRIBULATION PRECEDING THE DAY OF JEHOVAH

AFTER we have seen how fully the prophetic Word harmonizes in the revelation of the great day of Jehovah, we are prepared to follow throughout the Scriptures the events which cluster around that day, as well as the blessings which are promised to follow. As we continue in this we shall see more and more the perfect harmony of prophecy.

We point out first of all the fact that the entire prophetic Word gives us a minute description of the characteristics of the times which precede the manifestation of Jehovah in His day. In this description nearly all the different instruments through whom the Spirit of God spoke fully agree; nor does this description end with the Old Testament. It is continued in the New.

We touch now a most important theme of God's revelation. We are aware of the fact that what we shall learn from the Scriptures is in direct opposition to the beliefs and theories prevalent throughout Christendom. Alas! that so many who call themselves Christian believers should continue in these wrong conceptions and theories, and remain grossly ignorant of God's eternal purposes revealed in His Word. Men have taught and teach without any Scriptural warrant whatever, that a universal judgment day is to come, and that this day will come after the conversion of the world and the extension of the kingdom (as they term it) over the whole world. According to this almost universal belief, things are progressing favourably, improvements set in on all sides, evil is being rapidly checked, and the common lot of humanity improved; nations are purer than ever before, world-wide peace almost at hand, as well as the conversion of the great heathen nations. All this is an unscriptural dream, something which is completely against the revealed purposes of God. It is true there are many precious promises in the Scriptures which predict world submission, the complete rule of the King of kings over the nations of the earth, as well as peace on earth, but *nowhere* do we find these blessings predicted to come before the day of Jehovah, but throughout the entire prophetic Word the order is the reverse. *First* comes that great and terrible day of the Lord, and *then* world submission, the deliverance of groaning creation, and the nations will learn war no more. May it please our Lord to open the eyes and the hearts of many of His children to see these great fundamental truths.

The prophetic Word in its testimony harmonizes in respect to the characteristics of the times preceding the day of Jehovah. The characteristics announced by the prophets are: Evil, trouble, persecution, wickedness come to its climax, rebellious nations arising against God and against His Anointed, as well as upheavals of various kinds. When at last the Wicked One rules and the greatest darkness prevails, the day of Jehovah breaks in all its majestic grandeur.

The times preceding the day of Jehovah and His manifestation are everywhere described as days of trouble for God's earthly people, Israel, and for all the inhabitants of the earth.

In Genesis 15:12 we read:

"And when the sun was going down a deep sleep fell upon Abram, and lo, an horror of great darkness fell upon him."

This was done to announce unto Abram that his seed was to pass through a dark night, a horrible experience. The prophetic vision found its first partial fulfilment in Egypt. The end of that period, when the seed of Abraham was away from the land of promise, was the darkest, full of the severest sufferings. The captivity in Babylon was another national night experience for Israel, and now for well-nigh two thousand years the people whom God has not cast away are in a still greater dispersion. It will terminate like the other dispersions. The end will be, as it was in Egypt, by the intervention of God. However, before this will take place the seed of Abraham will pass through a dark night of suffering, called in different scriptures "the great tribulation."

One of the strongest types in the Old Testament foreshadowing Christ, His first and second coming, the salvation He brings for the Gentiles, and finally the blessings for His own who rejected Him, is Joseph. We read there of a famine which came upon the earth, and during that famine the sons of Jacob, who had sold their own brother, came face to face with him whom they had hated without a cause. The famine in the story of Joseph is typical of Israel's suffering yet to come in the great tribulation preceding the day of Jehovah.

We turn again to Moses' prophetic song in the 32d chapter of Deuteronomy.

As elsewhere in prophecy, the Spirit of God announces here the evil results of Israel's apostasy. According to the Song of Moses they were to apostatize.

> "Then Jeshurun grew fat and kicked—
> Thou art waxen fat,
> Thou art grown thick,
> And thou art covered with fatness;—
> He gave up God, who made him,
> And lightly esteemed the Rock of his salvation."
>
> (Deut. 32: 15.)

The Rock of his salvation is the Lord whom they rejected, and here Moses announces this fact. After these words, we read of their present dispersion. What a description of the calamities to come upon

them, and what a literal fulfilment of all up to the
twentieth century!

But we direct our attention mostly to the close
of this chapter:

"Vengeance is mine and recompense,
  For the time when their foot shall slip.
  For the day of their calamity is at hand,
  And the things that shall come upon them make haste,
  For Jehovah shall judge his people,
  And shall repent in favour of His servants,
  When He seeth their power is gone,
  And there is none shut up or left." (Deut. 32: 35, 36.)

Now, here we have a prediction which is still unfulfilled. It describes the condition of the chosen
people immediately before Jehovah intervenes in
their behalf. A calamity is to come upon them and
their power will be gone. Though Israel has passed
through many calamities, yet this great trouble,
when they shall be completely prostrated, has not
yet been reached. More than ever in our day Israel maketh flesh his arm and is departed from the
Lord; they trust in almost everything else except in
Him who is the Hope of Israel. They are then to
be plunged into trouble and sorrow before the Lord
arises for their deliverance.

But let us see if we find such prophecies in other
Scriptures.

We turn our attention next to the *Book of
Psalms.* These prophetic songs are especially rich
in predictions and vivid descriptions of the troubles

which come upon a remnant of the sons of Jacob. Many Psalms contain the experiences of the God-fearing part of the Jews passing through the tribulation and being delivered out of the hands of their enemies by the coming of the Lord from Heaven. We read of the dangers and perplexities by which this remnant, brought back to the land of their fathers, is surrounded. Their sufferings are clearly portrayed, and we hear their pleadings for divine mercy, deliverance, and interference. The imprecatory prayers, calling God's wrath down upon the enemies, are then in order, and will be answered by the majestic appearing of the heavenly King.

This is the only satisfactory key to these imprecatory Psalms, which call on God to destroy the enemies. Christians cannot use them, for we are to pray for our enemies. The pious Jews living in that time of trouble will utter these words.

We can confine ourselves to but a few of the many passages in the Psalms which speak of the days preceding the day and manifestation of Jehovah. To quote them all would take many pages.

As previously stated, the Psalms are divided into five books, corresponding to the five books of the Pentateuch. The Exodus part of the Psalms extends from Psalm 42 to 72. As we learn in the book of Exodus of Israel's bondage, suffering, tribulation, and miraculous deliverance, so we read in this second book of Psalms that which will befall Israel in the latter times, and their lot before the day of

Jehovah begins, as well as their deliverance by the intervening power of Jehovah.

The reader who is interested in a closer study of the final history of the remnant of Israel should read carefully the Exodus section of the Psalms. Here is the language of the believing remnant in trouble in the last days of this age:

> "Judge me, O God,
>   And plead my cause against an ungodly nation;
>   Deliver me from the deceitful and wicked man.
>   For thou art the God of my strength;
>   Why hast thou cast me off?
>   Why go I about mourning,
>   Because of the oppression of the enemy?"
>
> (Ps. 43: 1-2.)

We take another illustration:

> "Deliver me from mine enemies, O my God;
>   Secure me on high from them that rise up against me.
>   Deliver me from the workers of iniquity,
>   And save me from men of blood.
>   For behold they lie in wait for my soul;
>   Strong ones are gathered against me;
>   Not for my transgression, nor for my sin, O Jehovah."
>
> (Ps. 59: 1-3.)

It is very interesting and instructive to study these experiences, pleadings, and sufferings of the Jewish remnant in the coming days, the ending of our age, as revealed in the Psalms, and many are the lessons we can learn for ourselves, though we shall not be present on the earth when that day comes.

The book of *Joel,* as remarked before, speaks of the enemies of Israel under the type of the locusts. The 2d chapter contains a wonderful description of what is still unfulfilled. Before the Lord is merciful to His land and His people and restores all things, as well as pours out the Spirit upon all flesh, there will be an invasion of a hostile army into the land. This awful trouble is followed by the repentance of the people and their prayer, which reminds us of the many similar prayers in the Psalms:

> " Spare Thy people, O Jehovah,
> And give not Thy heritage to reproach,
> That the nations should rule over them,
> Wherefore should they say among the nations—
> Where is their God? "   (Joel 2: 17.)

This is at once followed by the coming of the day of Jehovah. He will answer His persecuted and outraged people out of heaven and appear himself for their deliverance.

> " *Then* Jehovah will be jealous for His land,
> And will pity His people.
> And Jehovah will answer and say to His people,
> Behold, I will send you the corn,
> The new wine and the oil,
> And ye shall be satisfied therewith:
> And I will no longer make you
> A reproach among the nations."   (2: 18, 19.)

The same revelation we can easily trace in the other prophets.

Hosea, for instance, contains a prophecy which is

48

in fullest harmony with Moses' song and the other prophecies:

> "I, I will tear and go away; I will carry off, and there shall be none to deliver. I will go away, I will return to my place, till they acknowledge their offence, and seek my face. *In their affliction they will seek me earnestly.* Come and let us return unto Jehovah: for He hath torn, and He will heal us; He hath smitten, and He will bind us up. After two days will He revive us: on the third day He will raise us up, and we shall live before His face" (Hosea 5: 14; 6: 1-3.)

In this passage we have the entire history of Israel in a nutshell. Jehovah had been with them, but on account of their unbelief had left them. However, He does not leave them forever. They are to acknowledge their offence and seek His face. When will it be? In their affliction. The history of the Jews, since they cried, "His blood be upon us and upon our children," has been a history of continued affliction, of blood and tears; yet have they not acknowledged their offence. They have not acknowledged their blood-guiltiness, as David did. (Psalm 51: 14.) A greater affliction is coming for that nation. The affliction here in Hosea is the great end affliction, the calamity in Moses' song, when their power is gone, and Jehovah will come in His own day, the third day, to raise up His people.

The Spirit of God unfolds the same characteristic of the last days in the vision of *Isaiah*.

The end of the 10th chapter gives us a description of these events. The Assyrian falls into the land, and wherever he marches there is trouble, bloodshed, and misery. He comes to the very hill of Jerusalem, where he is arrested by the Lord (chapter 10: 24-34). The Assyrian of the past is the prophetic type of the Assyrian of the future, one who invades Israel's land from the north.

In the 24th chapter of Isaiah we have a description of the day of Jehovah, and in the 25th we read the praise of the believing part of Israel in having escaped the terrible upheavals:

"For thou hast been a fortress to the poor, a fortress for the needy in his distress, a refuge from the storm, a shadow from the heat, for the blast of the *terrible ones,* as a storm against a wall. Thou hast subdued the tumult of strangers, as the heat in a dry place; as the heat by the shadow of a cloud, so the song of the terrible ones is brought low" (Isa. 25: 4, 5).

Turning to the 59th chapter we read the following prophecy:

"When the enemy shall come in like a flood, the Spirit of Jehovah will lift up a banner against him. And the Redeemer will come to Zion, and unto them that turn from transgression in Jacob, saith Jehovah" (59: 19, 20).

In Romans 11 we find a great New Testament witness concerning the future of the Jewish race. Their national conversion in a future day is maintained in that chapter. The Holy Spirit uses this very passage: "The Deliverer shall come out of Sion; He shall turn away ungodliness from Jacob" (Rom. 11:

26). It is evident then before the Deliverer comes, the enemy comes in like a flood. The enemy rushes in immediately before the Lord comes as Deliverer for His people.

The 60th chapter gives another prophecy of the same nature:

> "Arise, shine; for thy light is come, and the glory of Jehovah is risen upon thee. For, behold, *darkness* shall cover the earth, and *gross darkness* the peoples; but Jehovah will arise upon thee, and His glory shall be seen on thee."

It is clear that when Jehovah is revealed with His glory in His day, not light, but darkness, will cover the earth.

In the prophet *Jeremiah* we have, almost in the centre of the book, a number of chapters which treat of the future of Israel. The first one is the 30th, and here in the beginning we find the great tribulation for Israel announced as it is to take place in the last days:

> "And these are the words that Jehovah hath spoken concerning Israel and concerning Judah. For thus saith Jehovah: We have heard a voice of trembling, there is fear and no peace. Ask ye now, and see whether a male doth travail with child? wherefore do I see every man with his hands on his loins, as a woman in travail, and all faces are turned into paleness? Alas! for that day is great, so that none is like it; it is even the time of Jacob's trouble; but he shall be saved out of it" (Jer. 30:4-8).

In the prophet *Ezekiel* the Lord declares: "I will overturn, overturn, overturn it; and it shall be

no more, until He come whose right it is; and I
will give it Him" (21:27). Here, too, we have a
passage which clearly indicates the characteristic
of the end of the age. It will be overturning till
He comes whose right it is, the Son of Man, in
power and glory.

The Book of *Daniel* contains perhaps the com-
pletest prediction of this characteristic of the days
preceding the Return of the Lord:

"And at that time shall Michael stand up, the great
prince who standeth for the children of thy people: and
there shall be a time of distress, such as never was since
there was a nation until that time. And at that time thy
people shall be delivered, every one that is found written in
the book" (12:1).

It is obvious that this great distress must fall into
the future, for the people of Daniel have not yet
seen the deliverance promised in the context, nor
has Michael, the great prince, stood up for the
people. (Compare with Rev. 12:7.) The New
Testament throws complete light upon this passage.
We shall come to it later.

We quote but a few more passages. *Micah, 7:*
1-7, describes the evil day when the godly man is
no longer in the land; the day of visitation and
their perplexity has come. *Habakkuk* in his vision
saw that day of distress and the enemy coming in
like a flood, and thus he expressed himself:

"I heard and my belly trembled;
My lips quivered at thy voice;

THE GREAT TRIBULATION

Rottenness entered into my bones,
And I trembled in my place,
That I might rest in the day of distress,
When their invader shall come up against the people
    (Hab. 3: 16).

In the last chapter of *Zechariah* we have a description of the great siege of Jerusalem, which forms the culminating point of that great day of trouble. Just before Jehovah comes to fight against the nations Jerusalem will be in the greatest distress. History has nothing to show in the way of fulfilment of the last chapter of the prophet of Glory.

And if we turn to the New Testament we find that here, too, the same revelation is given.

In His Olivet discourse—by far the greater part of it relating to this future history, the end of this age, all yet to be fulfilled—our Lord spoke the following words:

"Then shall there be great tribulation, such as has not been from the beginning of the world until now nor ever shall be; and if those days had not been cut short, no flesh had been saved; but, on account of the elect, those days shall be cut short" (Matt. 24: 21, 22).

Let us remember that the Jewish disciples of our Lord do not represent the church. No church was then in existence. The question of the disciples was concerning the end or completion of the age. As they had absolutely no knowledge of the present age, the church age, they meant nothing else than the Jewish age. And the Lord gives them an answer accordingly. He refers them to the prophecy of Daniel (verse 15). The description He gives of the sufferings and tribulations of a faithful Jewish remnant, which keeps the Sabbath, harmonizes fully with what we have learned from the Old Testament. The above passage, in which our Lord speaks of the great tribulation, has nothing to do with the church. The elect are a remnant of God's earthly people. The days of that tribulation will be shortened, not to keep them from losing eternal salvation, but to save them in the earth so that they may form the nucleus of the kingdom.

" Immediately after the tribulations of these days the sun shall be darkened . . . they shall see the Son of Man " (verses 29, 30). The great tribulation thus precedes the visible coming of the Son of Man.

In the Epistles, which contain the truths for this present age, which is not Jewish, we look in vain for any passages which speak of *the* great tribulation. It is true tribulations are mentioned, but nowhere is the believer in Christ warned to look out for the great tribulation. The church has nothing whatever to do with that coming period of distress. She is taken away from the earth immediately before that tribulation begins.

In the Revelation, the last book of the New Testament, our Lord gives from above a continued description of the tribulation and distress at the end of the age. Before these mighty scenes of trouble are pictured, and the riders gallop over the earth to reap their awful harvest, the glorified church is seen in Heaven before Him who sits upon the throne (Rev. 4 and 5). The promise given in the third chapter has been fulfilled: "I will keep thee out of the hour of trial." It would lead us too far to describe all which we read in the chapters which follow the fifth. The aspect of all is intensely *Jewish*. It connects closely with the Old Testament predictions. Perhaps every scene of trouble and wrath mentioned in Revelation is found somewhere in the prophetic Word.

IV

THE NATIONS THE ENEMIES OF IS-
RAEL — THEIR FINAL OPPOSITION
TO JERUSALEM FOLLOWED BY
JUDGMENT UPON THEM

THROUGHOUT the Word a clear distinction is made
between the nation and the nations. The special
nation which God has chosen for Himself is the
seed of Abraham, or, as we generally term that
people, Israel. "You only have I known of all the
families of the earth" (Amos 3:2). "Ye shall be
a peculiar treasure unto me out of all the peoples—
for all the earth is mine—and ye shall be to me a
kingdom of priests, and a holy nation" (Exod.
19:5, 6). "Jehovah took pleasure in thy fathers,
to love them, and He chose their seed after them,
even you, out of all the peoples, as it is this day"
(Deut. 10:15). "Thus saith Jehovah, who giveth
the sun for a light by day, the ordinances of the
moon and of the stars for a light by night, who
stirreth up the sea so that the waves thereof roar—
Jehovah of Hosts is His name: If those ordinances
depart from before me, saith Jehovah, the seed of
Israel also shall cease from being a nation before
me for ever" (Jerem. 31:35). "God's gifts and
calling are without repentance" (Rom. 11).

But Israel was disobedient and became apostate. The times of the Gentiles, or nations, began then, and they are still running. Israel as a nation is set aside and the dominion of the earth is in the hands of the Gentiles.

"And now I have given all these lands into the hands of Nebuchadnezzar, King of Babylon, my servant; and the beasts of the field also have I given him to serve him. And all the nations shall serve him, and his son and his son's son, until the time of his land also come, when many nations and great kings shall reduce him to servitude." (Jer. 27:6, 7.)

Thus it was predicted through Jeremiah. Then Nebuchadnezzar had his dream of the great image, representing the four great world powers down to their final history (Dan. 2), and Daniel had his vision in which the history of the times of the Gentiles ending with the coming of the Son of Man in clouds, is revealed (Dan. 7). The Gentile world powers as seen by Nebuchadnezzar, the golden head, are four, the last divided into ten kingdoms; as revealed to the prophet Daniel in the form of beasts, they are likewise four. Zechariah in his night visions saw four horns, concerning which the Lord says: "These are the horns which have scattered Jerusalem, Judah, and Israel" (Zech. 1:19). These four horns are in harmony with the dream of Nebuchadnezzar and the vision of Daniel. They all describe the four great world powers. The prophet Joel in describing the locust plague which had devastated the land mentions four species of the insect, or rather the locust in its fourfold development, a type again of the four great Gentile powers who were to prey upon Israel's land during the time of their apostasy.

Everywhere these nations are described as the enemies of Israel, and therefore the enemies of God. The enmity of the nations against Israel, however, appears fully developed at the end of the age. When the Lord, Jehovah, at last arises, He comes to judge these nations for the evil they have done to His people and to Immanuel's land. The nations, though they have become "civilized" and call themselves "Christian nations," have sinned and are sinning against the chosen people. They have persecuted them and stripped them again and again. The worst, however, is yet to come.

If we turn once more to Balaam's inspired parables, we read there of the invincibility of the people whom Balaam and Balak the Gentile would have cursed:

> "For there is no enchantment against Jacob,
> Neither is there any divination against Israel.
> In its time it shall be said of Jacob and Israel,
> What God hath wrought!
> So, the people will rise up as a lioness
> And lift himself up as a lion." (Num. 23:23, 24.)

And so in Moses' song we read of the enemies of Israel whom the coming Jehovah judges.

The *Book of Psalms* is full of prophetic descriptions of the enemies of Israel and the believing remnant; their prayers for the overthrow and destruction of these enemies are then not only timely but will also be answered.

The 2d Psalm finds then its great fulfilment:

> " Why are the nations in tumultuous agitation
> And why do the peoples meditate a vain thing?
> The kings of the earth set themselves
> And the princes plot together
> Against Jehovah and against His anointed.
> Let us break their bands asunder
> And cast away their cords." (Ps. 2: 1-3.)

This will be the final attitude of the nations, and in our day we see already much of this spirit. In the 46th Psalm, that glad redemption song of the delivered nation, we see them looking back to what had been. " The nations raged, the kingdoms were moved " (verse 6).

Here is a prophetic picture of what has been and is yet to be:

> "O God, the nations are come into Thine inheritance,
> Thy holy temple have they defiled;
> They have laid Jerusalem in heaps.
> The dead bodies of Thy servants
> Have they given to be meat
> Unto the fowls of the heavens, the flesh of Thy saints
> Unto the beasts of the earth:
> Their blood have they shed like water
> Round about Jerusalem.
> And there was none to bury them." (Ps. 79: 1-3.)
>
> (Compare this with Rev. 11.)

But one more illustration from the Psalms. A prayer which will be heard from Jewish lips:

> "O God, keep not silence;
> Hold not Thy peace and be not still, O God:
> For behold Thine enemies make a tumult
> And they that hate Thee lift up the head
> And consult against Thy hidden ones;
> They say, Come, and let us cut them off from being
> a nation
> And let the name of Israel be mentioned no more.
> For they have *consulted together* with one heart;
> They have made an *alliance* together against Thee."
>
> (Psalm 83: 1-6.)

From these passages we learn then that the nations are not alone the enemies of God's chosen earthly people, but that at the end, immediately before the King is enthroned upon Zion's hill, they will band themselves together, and, consulting together, they will form an unholy alliance against His people, against God, and His Anointed. It is true, history shows in the past such conspiracies of nations against the chosen nation, but the great and powerful alliance of the nations is yet to come.* It falls in the period which we described in the last chapter, the great tribulation.

The book of *Joel,* which begins with the description of the locusts, literal locusts, which had played such havoc with the trees and all vegetable life, re-

* There will be a double confederacy of nations: the confederacy of the nations belonging to the restored Roman Empire, and the confederacy of the nations coming from the north under the leadership of the King of the North.

veals under the type of locusts an invasion of the
land by enemies. They are coming upon the land
from the north, and are called "the northern
army."

This invasion is described, perhaps, in the sub-
limest language ever used by any prophet.

> "Before them consumeth a fire
> And behind them a flame burneth;
> Like the garden of Eden the land is before them,
> And behind them—a desolate wilderness.
> Surely nothing escapeth them.
> The appearance of them is like the appearance of horses,
> And like horsemen shall they run.
> Like the noise of the chariots, on the tops of the moun-
> tains they leap;
> Like the noise of a flame of fire consuming stubble,
> Like a strong people set in battle array.
> Before them the people are trembling;
> All faces turn pale.
> They shall run like mighty men;
> They shall climb the wall like men of war:
> And they shall march every one in his ways,
> And shall not break their ranks.
> Neither shall one press upon another;
> They shall march every one in his path;
> And they rush upon the weapon, but shall not be wounded.
> They shall run around in the city;
> They shall run upon the wall;
> They shall climb up into the houses,
> They shall enter in at the windows like a thief.
> Before them trembleth the earth,
> The heavens shake,
> Sun and moon shall be darkened,
> And the stars withdraw their shining." (Joel 2: 3-10.)

When this awful invasion takes place, and Israel's land suffereth the worst, Jehovah will utter His voice and the enemies will be overthrown by His power.

> " And I will remove far off from you the northern army
> And will drive him into a land barren and desolate.
> His face towards the eastern sea,
> And his rear towards the hinder sea;
> And his stench shall come up,
> And his ill odours shall come up,
> For he hath exalted himself to do great things."
>
> (Joel 2:20.)

This northern army will be under the leadership of the King of the North, of whom and his allies we will hear in the next chapter. The 3d chapter in Joel describes the judgment of the nations who came up against Jerusalem. They will be brought down into the valley of Jehoshaphat and the judgment will be on account of Israel.

> " I will enter into judgment with them there
> On account of my people and mine inheritance Israel,
> Whom they have scattered among the nations:
> And they have parted my land,
> And they have cast lots for my people,
> And have given a boy for a harlot
> And sold a girl for wine and drunk it." (Joel 3:2-4.)
>
> . . . . "Let the nations rouse themselves
> And come up to the valley of Jehoshaphat,
> For there will I sit to judge all the nations round
>   about." (3:12.)

In the prophet *Amos* we find predictions against nations. This prophet began his prophetic office

by pronouncing judgment against the enemies of
Israel. They had sinned against Israel and done
evil to them. There has been a fulfilment unques-
tionably of these judgments, yet a final fulfilment
of it is yet to come. *Obadiah's* vision is about
Edom. Here, too, we read of a confederacy of
nations rising up against Israel.

Isaiah's vision contains many vivid descriptions
of the nations, their final onslaught on Jerusalem,
as well as their complete overthrow and judgment
by Jehovah's intervention and manifestaion. In the
first part of Isaiah the great event of the Assyrian's
invasion, coming from the north, and the miraculous escape of Jerusalem, as well as the destruction
of Sennacherib's army, form the basis of the prophecy. It is typical history of what shall be repeated,
only on a grander scale, before Jehovah comes. In
this light the 10th chapter is to be read.

With the 13th chapter begins a series of predictions against the nations. The first and most
prominent is Babylon, the last is Tyre. These utterances will find their literal fulfilment in the end of
this age. Babylon's past judgments have never
amounted to that which is declared in the thirteenth
chapter:

"And Babylon, the glory of the kingdoms, the beauty of
the Chaldees' excellency, shall be as when God overthrew
Sodom and Gomorrah. It shall never be inhabited, neither
shall it be dwelt in from generation to generation." (Isaiah
13: 19, 20.)

In the 29th chapter Jerusalem is called Ariel. "Ariel (the lion of God), the city where David dwelt." Here we find, first of all, a description of that great end drama of this age:

"I will distress Ariel, and there shall be sorrow and sadness and it shall be unto me as an Ariel. And I will camp against thee round about, and will lay siege against thee with watchposts, and I will raise forts against thee. And thou shalt be brought low, thou shalt speak out of the ground, and thy speech shall come low out of the dust and thy voice shall be as of one that hath a familiar spirit, out of the ground, and thy speech shall whisper out of the dust, and the multitude of thine enemies shall be like small dust, and the multitude of the terrible ones as chaff that passeth away; and it shall be an instant suddenly. Thou shalt be visited by Jehovah of hosts with thunder and with earthquake and great noise, with whirlwind and tempest, and the flame of devouring fire. And the *multitude of all the nations* that war against Ariel, even all that war against her and her fortifications and that distress her, shall be as a dream of a night vision. It shall even be as when the hungry dreameth, and, behold he eateth; and he awaketh, and his soul is empty; or as when the thirsty dreameth, and behold he drinketh, and he awaketh, and behold he is faint, and his soul craveth; so shall the multitude of *all the nations* be that war against mount Zion." (Chap. 29: 1-8.)

It is, of course, impossible to give a complete exegesis of this most interesting prophecy. We have put "all the nations" in italics, because it has been claimed that this prediction was long ago fulfilled. The term "*all nations*" and the multitude of all the nations points clearly to the future. Suffice it to say that this passage is in the closest har-

mony with what we have learned so far and what
we shall yet find concerning the ending of the age,
and the nations' attitude towards Jerusalem.

We take another prediction from the 34th
chapter:

" Come near, ye nations, to hear; and hearken, ye peoples,
let the earth hear and all its fulness; the world and all that
cometh forth of it. For the wrath of Jehovah is against
all the nations, and His fury against all their *armies*. He
hath devoted them to destruction; He hath delivered them
to the slaughter; and their slain shall be cast out, and their
stink shall come up from their carcasses, and the mountains
shall be melted with their blood." (34: 1-3.)

Other prophecies in Isaiah relating to this final
great conflict might be quoted, but these are sufficient. The very last verse in Isaiah is to be connected with the above quotation from the 34th
chapter:

" And they shall go forth, and look upon the carcasses of
the men that have transgressed against me; for their worm
shall not die, neither shall their fire be quenched; and they
shall be an abhorring to all flesh." (Isa. 66:24.)

These are the carcasses of the slain of the Lord
in that day.

Jeremiah is not silent concerning the nations and
their opposition to Jerusalem. Passing over a number of passages we quote the following:

" And I will bring upon that land all my words which I
have pronounced against it, all that is written in this book
which Jeremiah has prophesied against all the nations. For

many nations and great kings shall serve themselves of them also; and I will recompense them according to their deeds, and according to the work of their hands. For thus hath Jehovah the God of Israel said unto me: Take the cup of the wine of this fury at my hand, and cause all the nations to whom I send thee to drink it. And they shall drink and reel to and fro and be mad, because of the sword I will send among them." (Jer. 25: 13-17.)

Not for a moment would we say that there has not been a partial fulfilment of this, as well as similar passages. But the first captivity of Israel in Babylon is typical of their second and greater dispersion, in which they are now, and the announcements of Jehovah's coming in vengeance upon the enemies of His people reach on to the final great deliverance and restoration of His people.

The 50th and 51st chapters in Jeremiah describe the judgments to come upon Babylon, the fulness of which will be realized in the future. In the third part of *Ezekiel* (chapters 32-48), which treats of the coming restoration of the house of Judah and the house of Israel, and which contains so many precious promises to Israel and a description of their literal fulfilment, contains also a prophecy about the nations, especially Gog and Magog, which fall into the land immediately before the time of Jehovah's remembrance of His people. The dreadful end of these invaders is described. The reader will find this prophecy in the 38th and 39th chapters. The preceding chapter makes known the complete restoration of His people in the vision

of the resurrection of the dry bones. These enemies are " Gog, Magog, prince of Rosh, Meshech,
and Tubal." They are accompanied by other nations, " Persia, Cush, and Phut, with them, Gomer
and *all his bands;* the house of Togarmah from the
uttermost north, and all his bands, *many nations*
with thee."

From this we learn again the wonderful harmony
of these prophecies. Here, as we have seen in the
other passages, a confederacy of nations is accomplished before the day of Jehovah, and these nations
come down upon the land. That the land of the
north and the immense territory acquired by that
land—we mean Russia—will be in that confederacy
is obvious.* And now let us listen to the word of
prophecy concerning the final onslaught of these
enemies:

"And thou shalt come from thy place out of the uttermost north, thou and many peoples with thee, all of them

* "Rosh" certainly reminds one of "Russia"; "Meshech"
of "Moscow"; "Tubal," of "Tobolsk"; and "Togarmah,"
of "Turcomenia." Gog, Gomer, Meshech, etc., are first mentioned in Genesis 10. They settled in a northern direction.
Gog and Magog occupied the territory of Russia of to-day,
while Gomer was west of Gog and Magog, covering the
territory of Austria and Germany. It is a most interesting
fact that Russia is aware of this prophecy. Many intelligent
Russians believe Ez. 38:39 to mean their land. When the
first edition of this volume was published, a Russian prin-
cess ordered a copy. It was returned to the publisher, being
refused by the Russian censorship, the above passage being
the objectionable feature. Russia is the great Jew-hating
country.

riding upon horses, a great assemblage and a mighty army. And thou shalt come up against my people Israel as a cloud to cover the land, *it shall be at the end of days,* and I will bring thee against my land, that the nations may know me, when I shall be hallowed in thee, O Gog, before their eyes. Thus saith Jehovah: Art thou not he of whom I have spoken in old time *through my servants the prophets* of Israel who prophesied in those days, for many years, that I would bring thee against them? and it shall come to pass in that day, in the day when Gog shall come against the land of Israel, saith the Lord Jehovah, that my fury shall come up in my face; for in my jeaousy, in the fire of my wrath have I spoken. Verily in that day there shall be a great shaking in the land of Israel." . . . (Chap. 38:15-23.)

The overthrow of this hostile army and the terrible judgment which overtakes them is the theme of the 39th chapter:

"Thou shalt fall upon the mountains of Israel, thou and all thy bands, and the peoples that are with thee: I have given thee to be meat for the birds of prey of every wing, and to the beasts of the field. Thou shalt fall in the open field; for I have spoken it, saith the Lord Jehovah." (Chapter 39:3, 4, and to the end of the chapter.)

How complete the harmony with the other prophets! We may reach from here into the New Testament and quote a few verses of what John saw and heard in the isle of Patmos:

"And I saw an angel standing in the sun; and he cried with a loud voice, saying to all the fowls that fly in the midst of heaven, Come and gather yourselves together unto the supper of the great God; that ye may eat the flesh of kings, and the flesh of captains, and the flesh of mighty men, and the flesh of horses and of them that sit on them, and the flesh of all, free and bond, both small and great." (Rev. 19: 17, 18.)

This event takes place when the heavens open, and the King of kings comes forth, and is to be connected with the prophecy in the two chapters we quoted from in the book of Ezekiel.

Notice the fulfilment is to be at the end of days. It is also striking that the Lord saith in Ezekiel, 38: 17, " Art thou not he of whom I have spoken in old time through my servants the prophets of Israel?" Here then have we a full confirmation of what we said in the beginning. The Lord speaks Himself; the same Spirit through each of these men makes known God's purposes. Therefore this Divine harmony. How strange—that Christians can pass by these visions and prophecies and can pronounce them as being of little value! How wicked to say the Lord has not spoken, or to declare these sublime revelations to be the " imaginations of Jewish patriots "!

All readers of the Word know something of the great importance of the Divine revelations made to Daniel, the captive in the dispersion. It is not strange that both Jews and Gentiles should oppose and reject that greatest of all Old Testament prophetic books. The Jews have put Daniel in the Writings* and do not recognize Daniel as a prophet.

* The Hebrew Bible is divided into three parts: *Tora*, the Law; *Nevjim*, the Prophets; *Kethubim*, the Writings.

Of his wonderful prophecies they are sadly ignorant. Worse, however, is the way Higher Criticism has treated this book.

The great, final struggle in the land and around Jerusalem is here fully given. The prophecy of the seventy year-weeks is well known (chapter 9: 25-27). Jerusalem's history ends abruptly with the sixty-ninth week. It is, however, not fully ended. One week remains, the seventieth. The gap between the sixty-ninth and the seventieth week is the present age. This is of much importance. The present age, in which God by His Spirit forms the church, the body of Christ, is not a revelation contained in the Old Testament. As soon as this age is concluded, with the fulness of the Gentiles coming in, the completion of the church, Israel's history will begin again. The seventieth week will run its course, and in that week the times *of the Gentiles* * will terminate. This last week brings wickedness to the full; the great tribulation falls into that week; it is therefore entirely Jewish. Furthermore, in that last week the nations will fulfil their destiny under the leadership of the evil

---

* The times of the Gentiles are an entirely different thing from the "fulness of the Gentiles." A people is to be gathered out from the Gentiles for His name; when this is completed the fulness of the Gentiles is reached. The times of the Gentiles began *before* the calling out of a people for His name took place, and they will continue after the church is taken. The dominion of the Gentiles will end with the coming of the Lord visibly from Heaven.

ones by falling into the land. The events of this great period, the winding up of the day of man, and the beginning of the day of Jehovah, are contained in the last chapters of Daniel. It is not our intention to go through these chapters, as it would lead us into a more detailed exposition, which is not the object of this volume. The great war centering around Immanuel's land ends with the personal, visible, and glorious manifestation of the Son of Man.

The same testimony concerning the nations at the end of this age is found in Micah, chapters 4: 13; 5: 6; 5: 15; 7: 16-17.

Habakkuk stands personally as a type of the faithful remnant of God's people, struggling in faith and hope in the tribulation and conflict preceding the manifestation of Jehovah. In the 1st chapter we find a description of the Chaldean army and their invasion. While it is true that such an invasion took place in the past, it is also true that it stands for the coming greater invasion. The 3d chapter, to which we shall refer later, makes mention of this great, final struggle.

" They came out as a whirlwind to scatter me
  Whose exulting was as to devour the afflicted secretly."
  (Chapter 3: 14.)

In Zephaniah, chapter 2: 8-15 and chapter 3: 6 refer to the same judgment of nations. From Haggai we quote the following words:

71

"I will shake the heavens and the earth; and I will overthrow the thrones of kingdoms and I will destroy the strength of the kingdoms of the nations; and I will overthrow the chariots and those that ride therein; and the horses and their riders shall come down, every one by the sword of his brother." (Chapter 2: 21, 22.)

Next to the prophet Daniel, in the fulness of the revelation of these great future events, stands the prophet Zechariah.* In the first night vision he hears words from Jehovah which assure His gracious intervention in behalf of Jerusalem and words which denote His displeasure with the nations:

"Thus saith Jehovah of hosts: I am jealous for Jerusalem and for Zion with a great jealousy, and I am wroth exceedingly with the nations that are at ease; for I was but a little wroth and they helped forward the affliction." (Chapter 1: 14, 15.)

What an awful accusation that the nations helped forward the affliction!

We have before indicated that the four horns in the second night vision stand for the four world powers. (Chapter 2: 21.) This vision also shows that the horns of the nations are to be cast out. It is in the closing chapters of Zechariah we find many striking predictions of the nations coming against Jerusalem.

The 12th chapter contains several words of Jehovah relating to the closing scenes of the end of the age:

* For a complete exposition of this prophet of the coming glory see our book " Studies in Zechariah."

"Behold I will make Jerusalem a cup of bewilderment unto all the peoples round about and also against Judah shall it be in the siege of Jerusalem. And it shall come to pass in that day that I will make Jerusalem a burdensome stone unto all peoples; all that burden themselves with it shall certainly be wounded, and *all the nations of the earth* shall be assembled together against it" (12:2, 3).

"And it shall come to pass in that day that I will seek to destroy all the nations that come against Jerusalem" (12:9).

Still more is said in the last chapter of Zechariah. There we have the history recorded of the coming siege of Jerusalem. The historical fulfilment of the 14th chapter of Zechariah has often been attempted by critics, but they all have miserably failed. Though Jerusalem has seen many a siege, and perhaps more bloody and heartrending scenes than any other city of the world, but the siege prophetically described in the last chapter of the prophet Zechariah has not yet been. It is to come, and falls into the last half of the seventieth week of Daniel. It will form the awful climax of the great tribulation.

"Behold the day cometh for Jehovah, and thy spoil shall be divided in the midst of thee. And I will assemble *all nations* against Jerusalem to battle; and the city shall be taken, and the houses rifled, and the women ravished; and half of the city shall go forth into captivity; and the rest of the people shall not be cut off from the city.

"And Jehovah will go forth and fight with those nations, as when He fought in the day of battle. And His feet shall stand in that day upon the mount of Olives, which is before Jerusalem towards the east, and the mount of Olives shall cleave in the midst thereof towards the east and towards the west . . . and Jehovah my God shall come and all the holy ones with thee." (14: 2-5.)

In harmony with all the other prophetic predictions touching the punishment of these nations, we read in this wonderful *finale* of Zechariah the following:

"And this shall be the plague wherewith Jehovah will smite all the peoples that have warred against Jerusalem; their flesh shall consume away while they stand upon their feet, and their eyes shall consume away in their holes, and their tongues shall consume away in their mouth. And it shall come to pass in that day that a great panic from Jehovah shall be among them," etc. (Chap. 14: 12-15.)

Awful fate which awaits these nations! Little do the nations of Europe dream of what is in store for them. Little does Russia, and all with her, concern herself with her future divinely foretold. Antisemitism is growing everywhere, but the final great outbreak against Jerusalem is kept back by Him, who hindereth. The nations whose future and end is so clearly outlined in the prophetic Word call themselves even "Christian nations," possess the Bible, through which they may know God's purposes, and yet are ignorant of it all.

But how striking the harmony existing in the predictions concerning the nations at the end!

If we glance rapidly at the New Testament we find that the testimony of the theme of this chapter is continued there. Our Lord said to His disciples, "Jerusalem shall be trodden down until the times of the Gentiles be fulfilled." The last treading down of Jerusalem is at the end of the age. The great prophetic discourse of our Lord to which we have to refer again, contained in the 24th chapter of Matthew, reveals, as stated before, the events which take place immediately before His second visible coming in clouds in power and glory. Our Lord spoke elsewhere of the siege and destruction of Jerusalem in the year 70, but this siege is not before Him in the first part of Matthew 24. Here He speaks of the last siege, the siege of Zechariah 14, and pictures events which are far from being fulfilled at this time. In this chapter He speaks the familiar words:

"But you will hear of wars and rumours of wars. See that ye be not disturbed; for all these things must take place, but it is not yet the end. For nation shall rise up against nation, and kingdom against kingdom, and there shall be famines and pestilences, and earthquakes in divers places. But all these are the beginning of throes. Then shall they deliver you up to tribulation, and shall kill you, and you will be hated of all the nations for my name's sake." (Verses 6-9.)

Addressing these words to His Jewish disciples, representing the Jewish remnant, He tells them that the end of the age will be an end of tumult, political upheaval, and those who are then His faithful witnesses shall be hated by all nations. Later our Lord refers to the " abomination of desolation, which is spoken of through Daniel the prophet," and thereby calling our attention to this fact, that as Daniel's vision of the abomination of desolation (Dan. 9) falls in the end of the age, that His words likewise treat of the same period.

It is not a parable our Lord gives in the closing verses of the 25th chapter in the same Gospel. What He says there is the description of a great event following His glorious, visible advent at the end of the great tribulation, a description such as He alone could give.

"But when the Son of Man comes in His glory, and all the angels with Him, then shall He sit down upon His throne of glory, and *all the nations* shall be gathered before Him." (25:31-46.)

It is not a *universal* judgment of good and evil, believers and unbelievers, but a judgment of *all the nations*. The event follows His manifestion and is closely connected with prophecies like the one contained in the 3d chapter of Joel and others.

The book of Revelation after the 5th chapter is describing these struggles likewise as well as the judgments which fall upon Babylon, the kings and the nations. To follow all this in detail would take a volume for itself.

V

THE WICKED LEADERS OF THE APOS-
TATE FORCES AT THE END OF THE
AGE—THE ANTICHRIST

THE harmony of the Prophetic Word becomes still
more evident when we examine the revelation
that wicked ones will be the leaders of the confederacy of nations, and one will be the head
of the ecclesiastical apostasy. These leaders are
three. The Roman Empire, as seen in Nebuchadnezzar's dream, and Daniel's vision, will take on
the form of ten kingdoms, represented in Daniel's
vision by ten horns on the fourth, exceeding dreadful beast. Out of these ten horns a little horn
is to come forth; this little horn stands for the
head and leader of the revived Roman Empire in its
final form. The beast described in Revelation
17:8, "which was and is not and yet is," is the
Roman Empire. The second leader, *unquestion-
ably the most important* as well as the most wicked,
the very *incarnation of Satan,* is the personal *Antichrist,* the man of sin and the son of perdition, whose
perfect photograph we have in 2 Thess. 2, Rev.
13, Daniel 11, and other Scriptures. He is in
close alliance with the head of the Roman Empire,

only that the Antichrist assumes the place of the
leader of the ecclesiastical side of things. The
third is the *King of the North,* spoken of as another
little horn in Daniel 8:9, the Assyrian of the end
time. All three are moved by the same power,
Satan, have the same purposes, despising God and
His people Israel. It is true they are so much alike
that many readers of the Word do not see the distinction clearly, yet to have a clear view of these
three wicked persons is quite necessary for a more
complete understanding of Prophecy.

Now, if our object in writing this volume were
to study all prophetic passages analytically, we
would enter into these details, and give a closer
description of these three persons from Daniel and
Revelation. However, this is not our purpose, and
so we shall only show that the entire prophetic
Word speaks of this fact that at the consummation
of the age such evil persons will assume the leadership. We shall therefore not attempt a critical exposition to define the exact position and place they
will take.

The first promise given to Adam and Eve was
" He (the seed of the woman) shall crush thy
head and thou shalt crush His heel " (Gen. 3:15).
Christ first of all is the seed of the woman. The
crushing of the serpent's head will be fully carried
out when the Lord comes again, and when at last,
at the close of the day of the Lord, the old serpent,
the Devil, will be consigned to his eternal abode,

78

the lake of fire. Now, as Christ is the seed of the woman, and having a seed, so will the enemy have those in the earth who will be the heading up of all wickedness, the seed of the serpent. Like Christ, so has this wicked one his types. Pharaoh, Saul, Haman, Antiochus Epiphanes, Herod, as well as others, are clear types of these evil ones. We find him and his two associates mentioned throughout prophecy.

Balaam had to speak of him in his unwilling declaration of the future and glory of Israel. "His King," that is, Israel's King, "shall be higher than Agag, and His Kingdom shall be exalted" (Numbers 24:7). Agag is the title of the king of Amalek, and Amalek was the grandson of Esau, who appears as Edom in the prophetic Word. They stand for the flesh, and Agag as king stands here for the false king whose end will be when He comes whose right it is.

Moses in his song sees this dark and dreadful one looming up in his vision:

"Mine arrows will I make drunk with blood,
  And my sword shall devour flesh;
  I will make them drunk with the blood of the slain
  And of the captives,
  With *the head* of the princes of the enemy."

(Deut. 32:42.)

"The head" mentioned is the wicked one. If the Psalms are applied in dispensational light, and the afflicted, persecuted, and driven ones are seen to mean the faithful remnant of the Jews at the close of the age, we shall have no difficulty to find the wicked one, the enemy, fully described in them.

The 10th Psalm contains one of the first descriptions of the Antichrist:

> "His mouth is full of cursing, deceit, and oppression;
> Under his tongue is mischief and iniquity."
>
> (Ps. 10: 1-11).

The Psalms which follow up to the 15th Psalm are all descriptive of the condition of things when that wicked one will have the rule. Many other passages could be quoted in which a wicked one, a person, is mentioned, and a godly people suffering under his dreadful régime cries to Jehovah for deliverance. The following verses in the 37th Psalm may be read in this light, making known the comfort the remnant of His earthly people will have:

> "For yet a little while, and the wicked is not,
> And thou considerest his place, but he is not.
> But the meek shall possess the land.
> And shall delight themselves in the abundance of prosperity" (verses 10, 11).

The 43d Psalm shows us this evil person again. He is called in this Psalm "the deceitful and unrighteous man" (verse 1). Still more do we find of him in the 52d Psalm:

> "Why boasteth thou thyself in evil, thou mighty man?
> The loving kindness of God abideth continually.
> Thy tongue deviseth mischievous things;

Like a sharp razor practicing deceit.
Thou hast loved evil rather than good,
Lying rather than to speak righteousness.
Thou hast loved all devouring words,
O deceitful tongue!
God shall likewise destroy thee for ever;
He shall take thee away, and pluck thee out of thy tent,
And root thee out of the land of the living. Selah."

(verses 1-5.)

The 53d Psalm is almost like the 14th. While critics have found in this fact an argument for their unbelief in God's Word, we find in it a strong proof of the verbal inspiration. The 53d Psalm, standing in the second book of Psalms, occupies the same place which the 14th occupies in the first book. Like the 14th, the 53d describes the days of Antichrist in the earth: " Every one of them is gone back, they are together become corrupt; there is none that doeth good, not even one." It is complete apostasy. The 55th Psalm also refers to Antichrist: " He hath put forth his hands against such as are at peace with him; he hath broken his covenant " (verse 20). The 74th and 140th Psalms contain similar references.

We found in Joel the vision of the great army coming upon the land from the north. This army has at its head a King. He is called in chapter 2:20, " the Northerner," a person.

Edom, concerning which Obadiah had his vision, is a type of the Antichrist. It is he who is described and addressed in that prophet as a person:

"The pride of thy heart hath deceived thee, thou that dwellest in the clefts of the rock, whose habitation is high; he that saith in his heart, Who shall bring me down to the ground? Though thou exalt thyself as the eagle, and though thou set thy nest among the stars, thence will I bring thee down, saith Jehovah" (verses 3-4).

In the vision of Isaiah we find his person pictured as well as the important part he plays in the final scenes of this age, and his end. The Assyrian, whose invasion and complete destruction is so prominent in the first half of the book of Isaiah, is the type of the Assyrian of the end, the King of the North. God uses him to bring distress upon Jerusalem, but before the very gates of the city, in view of Zion, the hill of Jerusalem, he is broken to pieces. The whole 10th chapter from the 5th verse unfolds these coming events. The end of the chapter shows his advance upon Jerusalem. He comes to Nob, and shakes his hand against the mount of the daughter of Zion, the hill of Jerusalem. And then we read, "Behold the Lord, Jehovah of hosts, shall lop the boughs with violence; and the high ones of stature shall be hewn down, and the haughty ones shall be brought low" (chapter 10: 33). It is the sudden appearing of the Lord to punish the enemy of His people.

In the 11th chapter the Messiah as King is seen in His first and second coming. When He comes to judge the poor and reprove with equity the meek of the earth, He shall smite the earth with the rod of His mouth, and *with the breath of His lips shall*

WICKED LEADERS OF APOSTATE FORCES

He slay the wicked. The latter prophecy is applied
in the New Testament to the man of sin, the son
of perdition (2 Thess. 2).

In the 14th chapter we meet the wicked one once
more under the title "King of Babylon." The
Assyrian and the King of Babylon are different
persons. The King of Babylon stands for *the* beast
of the book of Revelation, the final head of the
world power, the head of the revived Roman Empire ruling in the final Babylon. The King of
Babylon of old is but a faint shadow of the dreadful King of the end. We read then a description
of his person and his fall:

"The whole earth is at rest, is quiet: they break forth
into singing. Even the cypresses rejoice at them, the cedars
of Lebanon, saying: Since thou art laid down, no feller
is come up against us. Sheol from beneath is moved for
thee to meet thee at thy coming, stirring up the dead for thee,
all the he-goats of the earth; making to rise from their
thrones all the kings of the nations. All of them shall
answer and say unto thee, Art thou also become as power-
less as we? art thou become like unto us? Thy pomp is
brought down to Sheol, the noise of thy lyres; the mag-
got is spread under thee and worms cover thee. How art
thou fallen from heaven, Lucifer, son of the morning! Thou
art cut down to the ground, that didst prostrate the nations!
And thou that didst say in thine heart, I will ascend into
the heavens, I will exalt my throne above the stars of
God, and I will sit upon the mount of assembly, in the
recesses of the north; I will ascend above the heights of
the clouds, I will be like the Most High: none the less art
thou brought down to Sheol, to the recesses of the pit.
They that shall see thee shall narrowly look upon thee, saying, Is this the man that made the earth to tremble, that

shook kingdoms; that made the world as a wilderness, and overthrew the cities thereof; that dismissed not his prisoners homewards?" (chapter 14:7-18).

The prophecy has often been applied to Satan himself, who was once Lucifer, "a brilliant star." However, it is to be explained that in these evil leaders, human beings, Satan will be manifested.

There are numerous passages in the book of Isaiah which speak of the Assyrian and his fate; all these refer us to the end and the punishment of the evil one, the last Assyrian:

"For through the voice of Jehovah shall the Assyrian be broken down; he will smite him with the rod . . . For Tophet* is prepared of old; for *the King* also it is prepared; he hath made it deep and large; its pile is fire and much wood; the breath of Jehovah, like a stream of brimstone, doth kindle it" (Isa. 30:31-33).

Here is his bitter end, and not alone his but that of the King as well, the false Messiah who comes in his own name and whom the Jews will accept. The authorized version has put the little word "*yea,* for the King" in the 33d verse and making it appear that the Assyrian is the King. But the King is the false Messiah, and his place will be in Jerusalem, the Assyrian is his enemy, but both will be cast into the lake of fire burning with brimstone (Rev. 19:20).

In chapter 57th is another prophecy quite often overlooked as having any reference to Antichrist, but it clearly has. The first nine verses of this

* 2 Kings 23:10.

chapter show the awful condition of the Jews in their final great apostasy. There is a King mentioned in the 9th verse to whom they go with ointment, before whom they worship. He is not the King of Israel, but the Satanic counterfeit of the King of kings.

While we have no fuller prophecies about the Antichrist and the others in Jeremiah such as we find in Isaiah, there are nevertheless several passages in which he is mentioned. We refer to chapters 23: 19, 30: 8, and 30: 23, 24.

In the prophet Ezekiel we call the attention especially to the 28th chapter. It is the word of Jehovah concerning the prince of Tyre. Such an arrogant prince reigned then, and there can be no question that the word of Jehovah had a special reference to that prince. But as we read carefully we find that his personality is a type of one who is to come, another prince. It is very striking that expressions which are used here by the Spirit of God concerning the prince of Tyre are repeated later by Him in the description of the Antichrist:

"Because thy heart is lifted up, and thou hast said, I am a god, I sit in the seat of God, in the heart of the seas (and thou art a man and not God), and thou settest thy heart as the heart of God: behold thou art wiser than Daniel! nothing secret is hidden from thee; by thy wisdom and understanding thou hast gotten thee riches, and hast gotten gold and silver into thy treasures: by thy great wisdom thou hast by thy traffic increased thy riches. Therefore thus saith the Lord Jehovah: Because thou hast set thy heart as the heart of God, therefore behold, I will bring strangers upon thee, the terrible of the nations; and they shall draw their swords against the beauty of thy wisdom, and they shall tarnish thy brightness. They shall bring thee down to the pit, and thou shalt die the deaths of those that are slain in the heart of the seas. Wilt thou then say before him that slayest thee, I am God? but thou shalt be a man and not God, in the hand of him that pierceth thee" (28: 1-8).

The remarkable statements we find in this passage and which are the signs and marks of the Antichrist are the following:

1. His heart is lifted up in pride.
2. He says, " I am God."
3. He takes his place in the seat of God.
4. He controls the sea and commerce.
5. He claims to be wiser than Daniel.
6. By his craftiness he gains riches.

It is the number " six," and as we have his number in Revelation 666—three sixes, meaning man in full opposition to God. We have, therefore, under the type of the prince of Tyre a perfect outline of the man of sin. Compare the above with the language of the Holy Spirit in 2 Thess. 2: 1-10.

His end is also very significant. He is to die the two deaths at once—" Thou shalt die the deaths."

And as we read what follows in the 28th chapter of Ezekiel, we become still more impressed with the deeper meaning of this prophecy:

"And the word of Jehovah came unto me, saying, Son of man, take up a lamentation upon the King of Tyre, and say unto him, Thus saith the Lord Jehovah: Thou who sealest up the measure of perfection, full of wisdom and perfect in beauty, thou wast in Eden the garden of God; every precious stone was thy covering, the sardius, the topaz, and the diamond, the chrysolite, the onyx, and the jasper, the sapphire, the carbuncle, and the emerald, and the gold. The workmanship of thy tambours and of thy pipes was in thee: in the day that thou wast created were they prepared. Thou wast the anointed, covering cherub, and I had set thee so: thou wast upon the holy mountain of God; thou didst walk up and down in the midst of the stones. Thou wast perfect in thy ways from the day that thou wast created till unrighteousness was found in thee (verses 10-19).

We see at the first glance that this description can fit but one person, and that is the fallen Lucifer, the son of the morning, Satan. As he stands in connection with the King of Babylon in Isaiah 14, as we saw above, so he stands here in relation to the prince of Tyre. It is Satan himself who acts through these evil ones. " The prince that is to come."—the King coming in his own name is Satan's revelation and masterpiece.

The fullest revelation of this subject is given in the prophet who received his visions in Babylon, the prophet Daniel. Not alone are here the minutest descriptions in prophetic visions of the three evil ones, but the historic events clustering around Daniel and his faithful companions are foreshadowings of the evil day and the awful persecutions to which the believing remnant of the Jews will be exposed under the régime of the false Messiah.

The great image which Nebuchadnezzar the King

set up in the plain of Dura is a type of another image which will be set up in Jerusalem, the image of the beast. And as in Daniel 3d, all were to be killed who refused to worship that image, so all who worship not the image of the beast shall be killed (Rev. 13). Thus all through Daniel the events have a highly typical and prophetic meaning.

It is, however, in the great prophetic visions and communications Daniel received we read of the two little horns and the Antichrist, the three terrible ones who will be revealed in the course of the last prophetic week of Daniel with which the times of the Gentiles close.

In the 2d chapter, Nebuchadnezzar's dream and its divine interpretation reveal the times of the Gentiles ending with the great catastrophe of the sudden destruction of the world powers. The 7th chapter contains the vision of the prophet concerning the same times of the Gentiles. The four great beasts arise out of the tumultuous sea, representing nations. The last, the fourth beast, was dreadful and terrible, exceeding strong; it had great iron teeth; it devoured and broke in pieces and stamped the rest with its feet; it was different from all the beasts that were before it, and it had ten horns. It corresponds with the two iron limbs of Nebuchadnezzar's dream image, and its ten toes mixed iron and clay represents the Roman Empire. This last Empire has passed out of actual existence, yet both the prophecy of Daniel and the book of Revelation show conclusively that it will be revived. Its revival will consist of ten kingdoms joined in a mighty western European confederacy. The beginning of the 13th chapter of Revelation speaks of this. The ten horns with their ten crowns are the same horns as revealed to Daniel.

Thus we read:

"I considered the horns, and, behold, there came up among them another, a little horn, before which three of the first horns were plucked up by the roots; and, behold, in this horn were eyes like the eyes of 'man, and a mouth speaking great things'" (Dan. 7:8).

The prophet sees after this thrones set and the books opened:

"I beheld till the beast was slain, and its body destroyed, and it was given up to be burned in the fire" (verse 11).

Then after the vision of the coming of the Son of Man from Heaven, the prophet desired to know the certainty concerning the fourth beast, the Roman Empire and the little horn. His desire is granted:

"He said thus: The fourth beast shall be a fourth kingdom upon the earth, which shall be different from all the kingdoms, and shall devour the *whole earth,* and shall tread it down, and break it in pieces. And as to the ten horns, out of this kingdom shall arise ten kings; and another shall arise after them; and he shall be different from the former, and he shall subdue three kings. And he shall speak words against the Most High, and shall wear out the saints of the most high places, and think to change seasons and the law; and they shall be given into his hand until a time and times and a half time [three and one-half years]. And the judgment shall sit, and they shall take away his

dominion, to consume and to destroy it unto the end"
(verses 23-26).

The little horn is generally called the Antichrist,
while many declare that as it refers to Rome, it
must be the Pope. However, this interpretation is
incorrect. Inasmuch as this little horn arises from
the revived Roman Empire and becomes the
domineering power of Rome in the end, the little
horn in Daniel 7 must be the head of that Empire,
the wicked leader of the western European confederacy of nations, the final King of Babylon, as
he is described in Isaiah 14. His character as
described here, his lawlessness and arrogant pride,
harmonizes fully with everything else as revealed
through the other prophets. It is likewise so as to
his end. "Given up to be burned with fire" (verse
11). "Thou shalt be brought down to Sheol, to
the sides of the pit" (Is. 14: 15). "And the beast
was taken, and with him the false prophet that
wrought miracles before him, with which he deceived them that received the mark of the beast, and
them that worshipped his image. These both were
cast alive into a lake of fire burning with brimstone"
(Rev. 19: 20).

We come next to the 8th chapter. Here we read
first of a great horn. The great horn was broken
and in its place came up four notable ones towards
the four winds of heaven. This prophecy was fulfilled in Alexander the Great, the great horn. But
out of one of these divisions came forth a *little horn*

which waxed exceeding great. Now this little
horn in Daniel 8 is not identical with the one in
the foregoing chapter. The little horn in chapter 8 rises out of the eastern parts of Europe.
That Antiochus Epiphanes and his abominations is
a partial fulfilment of the little horn seems clear.
Antiochus Epiphanes sprung from one of the four
kingdoms of Alexander's empire. But he typifies
also another person, a little horn which is yet to
rise in the northeast, and therefore the little horn
in Daniel 8 can be no other person than he who
is mentioned in the 9th chapter by the name
"King of the North." He is the Assyrian of the
prophet Isaiah, the Northerner of Joel. Antichrist
will be the enemy of the Jews in Jerusalem, the
Assyrian will press down upon the land and the
city from the north. To make one person out of
the two or to say that the little horn in Daniel 7
and the one in Daniel 8 is the same individual is
incorrect. But we must refrain from entering deeper
into this subject, interesting and most timely as it
is. And what then is said of this little horn?

"And out of one of them came forth a little horn, which
became exceeding great, towards the south, and towards the
east, and towards the beautiful land. And it became great,
even to the host of heaven; and it cast down some of the
host and of the stars to the ground, and trampled upon
them. And he magnified himself even unto the prince of
the host, and *from* him* the continual sacrifice was taken

* Notice the erroneous translation in the authorized version, "by him." It is from him the "prince of the host."

91

away, and the place of his sanctuary was cast down. And a time of trial was appointed unto the continual sacrifice by reason of its transgression. And it cast down the truth to the ground; and it practised and prospered. . . . And at the latter time of their kingdom, when the transgressors shall have come to the full, a king of bold countenance, and understanding dark sentences shall stand up (the above little horn). And his power shall be mighty, but not by his own power; and he shall destroy marvellously, and shall prosper, and shall practise, and shall destroy the mighty ones, and the people of the saints. And through his cunning shall he cause craft to prosper in his land; and he will magnify himself in his heart, and by prosperity will corrupt many; and he will stand up against the Prince of princes; but he shall be broken without hand." (The fate of the Assyrian.) (8: 10-13; 23-26.)

In the 9th chapter the coming evil one, the final head of the Roman Empire, is mentioned again. He is "the prince that shall come." "And he shall confirm a covenant with the many for one week; and in the midst of the week he shall cause the sacrifice and the oblation to cease, and because of the wing of the abominations there shall be a *desolator,* even until that the consumption and what is determined shall be poured out upon the desolator" (Dan. 9:27).

Turning to the wonderful 11th chapter we have in it a continued description of the evil one. Much of it refers to Antiochus Epiphanes; but at the close of the chapter is a prophecy which reveals the false Messiah, or, as he is generally called, the Antichrist, the man of sin and son of perdition:

92

WICKED LEADERS OF APOSTATE FORCES

"And the King* shall do according to his will; and he shall exalt himself and magnify himself above every god, and speak monstrous things against the God of gods; and he shall prosper until the indignation be accomplished; for that which is determined shall be done. And he will not regard the God of his fathers,† nor the desire of women, nor regard any god, for he will magnify himself above all" (verses 36-38).

So then in Daniel we have most comprehensive prophecies concerning the three awful individuals.

We refer now but briefly to a few passages in the other prophetic books. The 5th chapter of Micah predicts, with the exception of the 2d verse, which was fulfilled in the first coming of our Lord in humility, events still future. And here we have the Assyrian mentioned:

"And he shall stand and feed his flock in the strength of Jehovah, in the majesty of the name of Jehovah his God. And they shall abide; for now shall he be great even unto the ends of the earth. And this man shall be Peace when the Assyrian shall come into our land: and when he shall tread in our palaces," etc. (5: 4, 5).

In Nahum's burden of Nineveh we read of him. Sennacherib, the Assyrian, must have been meant first of all, but the Assyrian, the King of the North, forms the fulfilment of the prophecy:

* Called King because to be the false Messiah he will have to claim to be Israel's King.

† From this we would take it that while the chief of the Roman Empire and the King of the North are Gentiles, the false Messiah will be a Jew. The Jews will receive only a Jew as a Messiah.

93

"Out of thee is gone forth one that imagineth evil against Jehovah, one who has the wisdom of Belial.* Thus saith Jehovah: Though they be complete in number, and many as they be, even so shall they be cut down, and he shall pass away; and though I have afflicted thee (Israel) I will afflict thee (Israel) no more. And now I will break his yoke from off thee, and will break thy bonds asunder. And Jehovah hath given commandment concerning thee (the Assyrian), that no more of thy name be sown: out of the house of thy God will I cut off the graven image and the molten image. I will prepare thy grave: for thou art vile" (1: 11-14).

Habakkuk mentions that wicked one. He refers to him by the Spirit in connection with the coming of the Lord:

"Thou didst smite off the *head* of the house of the wicked,
Laying bare the foundation even to the neck" (3: 13).

The prophet himself trembles in view of the scenes which his prophetic vision beheld, and he says:

"I heard and my belly trembled;
My lips quivered at thy voice;
Rottenness entered into my bones,
And I trembled in my place,
That I might rest in the day of distress,
When their invader shall come against the people."
(3: 16.)

Zechariah speaks of the false Messiah as a foolish, worthless shepherd, and his punishment:

* It is most significant that the "wicked counsellor" of the authorized version is in the Hebrew—one who has the wisdom of *Belial.*

94

WICKED LEADERS OF APOSTATE FORCES

"For, behold, I will raise up a shepherd in the land, who shall not visit those who are about to perish, neither shall seek that which is strayed away, nor heal that which is wounded, nor feed that which is not sound; but he will eat the flesh of the fat, and tear their hoofs in pieces. Woe to the worthless shepherd that leaves the flock!" (11: 15-17.)

This, standing at the end of Zechariah, is in closest connection with the siege of Jerusalem, described in the 12th and 14th chapters.

Having rapidly glanced at these remarkable Divine predictions concerning the final leadership of the ungodly, apostate forces, and having seen their harmony, we point out the same revelation in the New Testament.

We must turn first of all to the Olivet discourse in Matthew 24. Our Lord answers the question of the disciples about the end of the age, which we hold, as stated before, to be the very end of the interrupted Jewish age. The first sign of this ending age He gives as the appearing of many who shall say, "I am the Christ." This is followed by wars, famines, pestilences, and earthquakes. If we turn to the 6th chapter in the book of Revelation, we find the same order of events in the opening of the seals. It is the beginning of the time of trouble. The first seal opened shows one upon a white horse, with a bow and a crown, and he goes forth to conquer. Strange that many interpreters make out of this one the Lord, or the universal preaching and conquest of the Gospel. But it is he who comes and says, "I am the Christ"; the false one.

Then in Matthew 24:15, we read of the abomination of the desolation spoken of by Daniel. Our Lord Himself refers to the passage in Daniel 9:27. It will be in the middle of the week that the abomination will be set up in Jerusalem.

In the Gospel of John our Lord speaks of the wicked one again when He says:

"I am come in My Father's name, and ye receive Me not; if another shall come in his own name, him ye will receive" (John 5:43).

The one to come and who will be received by the unbelieving Jews is the false Messiah. The book of Acts, the beginning of it, is a foreshadowing of the end of the age. As there was then only a Jewish remnant witnessing and suffering persecution, so it shall be again. King Herod, his awful persecutions and blasphemy, as well as his dreadful end, show clearly that he is a type of the wicked King to come (Acts 12).

Second Thessalonians, the 2d chapter, gives a fuller description of him. Here he is not only a false Messiah, but he also stands in relation to apostate Christendom. There is no question that after the church is removed and our gathering unto the Lord has taken place, that there will be an alliance between apostate Judaism and apostate Christendom. We see matters shaping themselves for it in

96

our own day. So then the evil one coming will be for the Jews the false Messiah, and for Christendom the Antichrist:

"Let not any one deceive you in any manner, because it will not be (the day of the Lord) unless *the* apostasy (in its final form) have first come, and the man of sin have been revealed, the son of perdition; who opposes and exalts himself on high against all called God, or object of veneration; so that he himself sits down in the temple of God, showing himself that he is God. Do ye not remember that, being yet with you, I said these things to you? And now ye know that which restrains that he should be revealed in his own time. For the mystery of lawlessness already works; only there is He who restrains now until He* be gone, and then the lawless one shall be revealed, whom the Lord Jesus shall consume with the breath of His mouth, and shall annul by the appearing of His coming; whose coming is according to the working of Satan in all power and signs and wonders of falsehood, and in all deceit of unrighteousness to them that perish, because they have not received the love of the truth that they might be saved" (2 Thess. 2:3-13).

It is needless to point out to the reader the perfect agreement which exists between this New Testament description and the many prophetic predictions of the Old Testament. Only the Spirit of God can produce such a harmony.

In the first Epistle of John the one who comes in his own name, the man of sin and son of perdition, is called the Antichrist. He has many forerunners, but at last the personal Antichrist will be manifested. He denies the Father and the Son.

* We write "He" with the capital "H" because we believe it refers to the Holy Spirit.

Space forbids to follow the final revelation of this trinity of evil persons as revealed in the last book of the New Testament. In it we have the whole Old Testament revelation, especially as given in Daniel, taken together, and the beasts and the false prophet are described in their actions, their wickedness, their end, as well as all that which is in connection with them (Rev. 13: 19). We must leave it to the reader to search and research these Scriptures, comparing Scripture with Scripture. Surely it is meat in due season. The time is near. All is getting ready for the manifestation of these masterpieces of Satanic cunning and power.

Yet none of us who are Christ's shall see that evil day with its evil leaders. Our feet shall be like hinds' feet, and we shall walk in our places (Hab. 3: 19).

VI

THE VISIBLE AND GLORIOUS MANIFES-
TATION OF JEHOVAH OVER THE
EARTH AND IN THE EARTH

FROM the dark scenes of the tribulation and the description of the evil persons playing such an important part at the close of the times of the Gentiles we turn next to the bright and wonderful prophecies relating to the visible and glorious manifestation of Jehovah. These prophecies, which reveal the opened heavens and out of these opened heavens coming forth with unspeakable glory a Divine person in the form of a man, like almost everything else in the prophetic Word, have been grossly spiritualized, or, as someone called it, "phantomized." All kinds of spiritual applications have been made from it; the most favoured is to see in it "the glory of the church." Others admire these prophetic descriptions as remarkable and highly poetical productions of the Jewish patriotic heart, etc. Strange, indeed, it is that but few believers throughout Christendom look upon all these promises of a personal, visible, and glorious manifestation of Jehovah, as real promises of God, as real as any promise contained in the New

Testament, and that all must be literally fulfilled.
Oh, how much such readers of the Word of God
miss in the joy of knowing the secret things of
Jehovah, He has been pleased to reveal to us! To
many it seems almost fabulous that all these
prophecies should be literally fulfilled, as if the Lord
is limited in His strength. Others again speak
of a visible manifestation of Jehovah as a too mater-
ialistic conception. These forget that Jehovah did
reveal Himself in the past, and that for a time His
glory was with His earthly people Israel. They
forget that the closed heavens during this age will
not be closed forever, and the silence of God existing for so long will at last be broken and He will
speak again.

And who is He of whom we read as Jehovah,
whose glorious person will be revealed? None
other than Jehovah-Jesus, the God-man, the Lord
of Glory. He is to come in His power and glory.
He is the One who created the worlds and the angels, who was made a little lower than the angels
in incarnation, and who, after He made purification
of sins by Himself and by resurrection declared
the Son of God in power, the first begotten from
the dead, went into the highest heavens, above the
angels, and sat down as the glorified Man at the
right hand of the Majesty on high. The Jehovah
whose visible and glorious manifestation we shall
follow in comparing Scripture with Scripture is our
Lord Jesus Christ.

VISIBLE MANIFESTATION OF JEHOVAH

There is much in the Old Testament besides the more direct prophetic predictions foreshadowing Jehovah's manifestation and the manner in which it will take place. There are, for instance, the Theophanies (Appearings of God). They not only foreshadow the first coming of our Lord, but also His second coming. We can only hint at a few of the many things which might be mentioned.

It is a well-known fact that Jehovah Himself dwelt with His people Israel and manifested His glory in their midst. With the presence of Jehovah there was associated an outward sign, which was a cloud: "And Jehovah went before them by day in a pillar of cloud to lead them the way; and by night in a pillar of fire, to give them light to go by day and by night." (Ex. 13:21.) Out of that cloud Jehovah looked upon the hosts of the Egyptians, and by that look they were troubled and confused. (Ex. 14:24.) The glory of the Lord appeared in that cloud. (Ex. 16:10.) The Lord descended in a cloud and stood before Moses. There was also the cloud upon the mercy seat. Jehovah came down repeatedly in a cloud (Numbers 11:25; 12:5, etc.), and later the glory of Jehovah filled the temple after Solomon's prayer, and that glory came in form of a cloud. All this is very significant and important for us to notice in these brief remarks, for it has much to do with the great coming manifestation of Jehovah.

If we turn to the book of Exodus, chapters 19

and 20, we find there the record of a manifestation of Jehovah to which the Holy Spirit refers repeatedly through the Prophets, and which is used
to foreshadow the coming glorious manifestation of
the Lord.   Here we read:

" And it came to pass on the third day when it was morning, that there were thunders and lightnings, and a heavy
cloud on the mountain, and the sound of the trumpet exceeding loud . . . and the whole of Mount Sinai smoked,
because Jehovah descended on it in fire; and its smoke
ascended as the smoke of a furnace, and the whole mountain shook greatly."   (Ex. 19: 16-18.)

In Deuteronomy Moses utters next to his prophetic song a blessing which undoubtedly will see
its fulfilment in the coming age when Israel is restored to the land.   In the beginning of the 33d
chapter we find a word which not only refers us to
the past but to the future as well.   As Jehovah is
described there rising up from Seir, shining forth
from Paran, coming with the myriads of the sanctuary, so will He come forth to bless Israel again.
And now as we look to the prophetic testimony
contained in the book of Psalms and the visions of
the prophets we shall find how clearly these outward signs of glory are given again and again, besides many other descriptions of the glorious manifestations of Jehovah, the Creator and Saviour,
Lord of lords and King of kings.

In the book of Psalms, where, as mentioned in
previous chapters, a future remnant of Jews is

seen suffering and waiting for deliverance by Divine interference, we find some of the most glorious descriptions of Jehovah's manifestation. In the 18th Psalm we have one which leans closely on the manifestation of Jehovah described in Exodus 19 and Deuteronomy 33. It is a superficial Bible study which can claim a fulfilment of this Psalm in the experience of King David. As far as we know he never had passed through an experience such as related in this Psalm. It is Christ first of all who is before us in this sublime song. He went into death and the deliverance was resurrection. But it is not Christ alone but also the remnant of His earthly people who will have to cry in the great tribulation: "The bands of death encompassed me, and the torrents of Belial made me afraid. The bands of Sheol surrounded me, the cords of death encountered me. In my distress I called upon Jehovah, and I cried unto my God. He heard my voice out of His temple, and my cry came before Him into His ears" (verses 4-6). This Psalm also stands at the close of David's history— signifying that it has to do with the end-history of David's seed. The description therefore which follows the pleadings for deliverance in the last days of the great tribulation can have only one meaning—the manifestation of Jehovah from Heaven visibly and in glory. If all these descriptions have such a marked resemblance to the events which took place when Jehovah delivered His peo-

ple out of Egypt and when He gave them the law,
it is a very simple indication that as Jehovah acted
then and appeared in glory, so will He act once
more and show His glory. Here then is the Spirit
of God witnessing to the great future event, looking on towards the future and giving it in the
language of a past event:

"Then the earth shook and quaked;
  And the foundations of the mountains trembled and shook,
  Because He was wroth.
  There went up a smoke out of His nostrils,
  And fire out of His mouth devoured:
  Coals burned forth from it.
  And He bowed the heavens and came down;
  And darkness was under His feet.
  And He rode upon a cherub, and did fly;
  Yea, He flew fast upon the wings of the wind.
  He made darkness His secret place;
  His tent round about Him;
  Darkness of waters, thick clouds of the skies.
  From the brightness before Him His thick cloud passed
      forth
  Hail and coals of fire.
  And Jehovah thundered in the heavens,
  And the Most High uttered His voice;
  Hail and coals of fire." (Verses 7-13.)

Sublime picture, is it not? It will all be fulfilled.

In the 29th Psalm we find another description
of the display of the power and majesty of Jehovah in His glorious day. It is the *voice* of Jehovah
which is made prominent here:

" The voice of Jehovah is upon the waters;
The God of glory thundereth:
Jehovah upon great waters.
The voice of Jehovah is powerful;
The voice of Jehovah is full of majesty.
The voice of Jehovah breaketh cedars;
Yea, Jehovah breaketh the cedars of Lebanon.
And He maketh them to skip like a calf;
Lebanon and Sirion like a young buffalo.
The voice of Jehovah cleareth out flames of fire.
The voice of Jehovah shaketh the wilderness;
Jehovah shaketh the wilderness of Kadesh.

(Ps. 29: 3-9.)

It is the manifestation of His person, and His voice will be heard. The 45th Psalm likewise describes Jehovah the King coming in His glory. What a Psalm it is! He who is addressed as God in this Psalm is also called " the fairest among the children of men," and it is said of Him, " Thou lovest righteousness and hatest wickedness." This has been fulfilled in our Lord, God manifested in the flesh. And He who was made a little lower than the angels, has received a throne and will have a sceptre, is described in this Psalm in His royal glory when He enters the earth again with His sword girded on His thigh, the victorious Conqueror who comes to rule the nations with a rod of iron. His beauty as the bridegroom is seen also in this song, the product of " the ready writer," the Holy Spirit.

The 50th and 68th Psalms give us additional descriptions of the glory of the coming of Jehovah, and in the 76th Psalm we read of it likewise. We cannot mention here all the other Psalms which predict Jehovah's manifestation at the end of Jacob's great trouble for the deliverance of the remnant of His earthly people.

In Joel we read that Jehovah shall utter His voice (3: 11), and the mighty ones come down with Jehovah in the earth when the nations are assembled, while the sun and the moon are darkened and the stars withdraw their shining.

Isaiah is rich and full of Divine predictions of what will be seen by the people Israel and the nations of the earth when the day of Jehovah comes. In the 2d chapter He is seen arising to shake terribly the earth, and it will be in the *glory of His majesty* (chapter 2: 19). In the 4th chapter the visible glory cloud which comes with Him as it surrounded Him when He dwelt with Israel is described, and we are told the glory will rest over Jerusalem. His sudden appearing is described in chapter 10: 33, 34. In chapter 11: 4 He comes to smite the earth with the rod of His mouth. Israel will welcome Him and say, " Lo, this is our God; we have waited for Him, and He will save us; this *is* Jehovah; we have waited for Him, we will be glad and rejoice in His salvation " (chapter 25: 9). In chapter 30: 27-30, we read:

"Behold, the name of the Lord cometh from afar, burning with His anger, a grievous conflagration: His lips are full of indignation, and His tongue as a consuming fire:

and His breath as an overflowing torrent, which reaches even unto the neck, to sift the nations with a sieve of destruction, and to put a bridle into the jaws of the peoples, that causeth them to go astray. . . . And Jehovah will cause the majesty of His *voice* to be heard, and will show the lightning down His arm with indignation of anger, and a flame of consuming fire, with water, flood and storm and hailstones."

And again it is promised to Israel: "Thine eyes shall see the King in His beauty" (chapter 33:17); "And the glory of Jehovah shall be revealed, and all flesh shall see it together; for the mouth of Jehovah has spoken it" (chapter 40:5). How often is the term "Glory of Jehovah" spiritualized. It means in this and in many other passages His outward glory, that glory of which He once emptied Himself. As He stood on the mount of transfiguration His glory was revealed. When He ascended and was received by the cloud in the heavens glimpses of the glory with which He comes back and which will be witnessed by all flesh were seen. But one more quotation from Isaiah:

"Who is this that cometh from Edom, with deep red garments from Bozrah? this that is glorious in His apparel, travelling in the greatness of His strength? I that speak in righteousness, mighty to save. Wherefore is redness in thine apparel, and thy garments like him that treadeth in the winefat? I have trodden the winepress alone, and of the peoples not a man was with me: and I have trodden them in mine anger, and trampled them in my fury; and their blood is sprinkled upon my garments, and I have stained all mine apparel. For the day of vengeance was in my heart, and the year of my redeemed was come." (63:1-4.)

Here the King of Glory is seen coming from the battle with His enemies.

Ezekiel in his 1st chapter describes the vision of the whirlwind and the great cloud and the fire. It is the vision of the glory of the Jehovah, which the prophet by the River Chebar beheld. The heavens were opened, and he saw visions of God. At the close of the 1st chapter we read what this glory of Jehovah was like:

"And above the expanse that was over their heads was the likeness of a throne, as the appearance of a sapphire stone; and upon the likeness of the throne was a likeness as the appearance of a man above upon it. And I saw as the look of glowing brass, as the appearance of fire, within it round about; from the appearance of his loins and upward, and from the appearance of his loins and downward, I saw as it were the appearance of fire, and it had brightness round about. As the appearance of the bow that is in the cloud in the day of rain, so was the appearance of the brightness round. This was the appearance of the likeness of the glory of Jehovah." (Ez. 1: 26-28.)

This then is the description of the glory of Jehovah. It was then leaving Israel. The visible sign of Jehovah's presence was leaving His people, but when He returns the King of Israel then His glory will be seen again welcomed by the glad worship song of His earthly people, "Blessed is He that cometh in the name of the Lord." In the closing chapters of Ezekiel we read of this returned glory:

"Afterwards he brought me unto the gate, the gate which looked towards the east. And, behold, the glory of the Lord of Israel came from the way of the east: and His voice was like the voice of many waters; and the earth was lit up with His glory. And the appearance of the vision that I saw was according to the vision that I had seen when I came to destroy the city: and the visions were like the vision that I saw by the river Chebar; and I fell upon my face." (Chapter 43:1-4.)

Daniel's familiar vision is well known, the coming of one like a Son of Man in the clouds of Heaven (chapter 7:13). It is the vision of the coming of Jehovah to rule and to reign over the earth.

In the 2d chapter of Habakkuk we find the promise of the glory of the Lord:

" For the earth shall be filled with the knowledge of the glory of Jehovah, as the waters cover the sea." (2:15.)

The previous verse declares what days all this shall take place. The people shall labour for the very fire and weary themselves for vanity, a prophecy the fulfilment of which is only too apparent in our day. It is in the 3d chapter where we find one of the finest descriptions of the visible and glorious manifestation of Jehovah. Habakkuk did *not* borrow, as some have said, from the description of the manifestation of Jehovah when He gave the law, or from other prophets, but the Spirit of God gives through him the same testimony concerning this great event as He did through His other chosen instruments. That there is a marked reference in this chapter to the manifestation at Sinai is seen at the first glance. It is an interesting fact that the orthodox Jews in keeping the feast of the Firstfruits read from the Law the chapter from Exodus which describes the manifestation of Jehovah at the giving of the Law, and from the prophets they read the 3d chapter of Habakkuk and the 1st chapter of Ezekiel. And now we quote part of this chapter (Hab. 3):

> "God comes from Teman,
> And the Holy One from mount Paran. Selah.
> His glory covereth the heavens,
> And the earth is full of His praise.
> And His brightness is like the sun;
> Rays stream from His hand;
> And there is the hiding of His power.
> Before Him goes the plague,
> And burning pestilence follows His feet.
> He stands and measures the earth:
> He looks and makes nations tremble;
> The everlasting mountains are broken in pieces,
> The eternal hills sink down:
> His ways are everlasting.
> I saw the tents of Cushan in trouble:
> The tent curtains of the land of Midian tremble.
> .   .   .   .
> The mountains saw thee, they writhe;
> A flood of water passes over:
> The abyss utters its voice,
> It lifts up its hands on high.
> Sun, moon stood back in their habitation,
> At the light of thine arrows which flew,
> At the shining of the lightning of thy spear.
> In anger thou marchest through the earth,
> In wrath Thou treadest down the nations."

We call attention to but one fact. The Holy

One who is here seen advancing, His glory flashing over the heavens and filling the earth with glory, has rays streaming forth from His hands. This is significant, for these hands were once outstretched on the cross and pierced. When He comes the nailprints will be visible, and from these hands emanates the glory now.

In the prophet of glory, the prophet Zechariah, His visible and glorious manifestation is pictured in a number of passages. In chapter 9:9, 10, He is seen as the coming King. Thus He came once to Jerusalem and was rejected; He will come the second time and be received. In chapter 12:10, the penitent nation looks upon the Holy One, upon Him whom they have pierced, and in the last chapter we read that His feet will stand in that day, in the day of Jerusalem's extremity, upon the Mount of Olives. It will be the day of Jehovah's visible manifestation, and not only His manifestation, but the manifestation of His saints as well. "And Jehovah my God shall come; all the saints with thee" (Zechariah 14:5).

The last book of the Old Testament speaks of this glorious manifestation as the rising of the Sun of Righteousness with healing beneath His wings. In this picture the Holy Spirit gives us a faint indication of what His visible manifestation will be —Brightness, Glory, and Power.

The testimony of the Spirit in the New Testament is not different from His witness in the Old

at which we have glanced in this chapter. All
the descriptions of Jehovah's outward glories, His
majestic appearing, the cloud of glory accompanying
Him, His voice, His brightness greater than the
sun, His work in judgment, and His mercy in
wrath are all repeated. We learn, above all, that it
is our Lord Jesus Christ to whom all applies, and
that the fulfilment falls in the day of His visible
return to the earth. To quote here the passages
contained in the New Testament, which so fully
harmonize with the predictions in the prophets and
the Psalms, is an impossibility. We call the attention to but a few facts. Our Lord in speaking of
His return as Son of Man always mentions the outward glory and that He will come in power. In
Matthew 16 He reveals for the first time His death
and resurrection, but He also speaks of His glory:
"For the Son of Man shall come in the glory of
His Father with His angels; and then shall He re-
ward every man according to His works. Verily
I say unto you, There be some standing here which
shall not taste of death till they see the Son of man
coming in His kingdom." (Matt. 16:27, 28.)
The last verse is to be brought in connection with
the transfiguration which followed six days later
(Matt. 17), and which is, as we have stated from
2 Peter 1 in our introduction, a foreshadowing of
our Lord's coming in His kingdom. And there
He stood as Son of Man in His glory, His face
shining like the sun, His raiment white as the

light. And there was also the *bright cloud,* the Shekinah cloud, the cloud which tarried once with Israel, the cloud in which Jehovah descended in olden times, the cloud which Ezekiel saw departing and returning. In Matthew 24: 30, He speaks of the signs of the Son of Man which shall appear in the heavens. It will be the bright cloud which the remnant of Israel will recognize at once as the sign of Jehovah's presence. Then shall all the tribes of the land, Israel's land, mourn, and they shall see the Son of Man coming in the clouds of Heaven with power and great glory.

In the book of Acts we read of His ascension. He was taken up and it was a cloud which received Him out of their sight. The event took place on the Mount of Olives. Still gazing upward, the disciples heard the words of the two men in white apparel: "Ye men of Galilee, why stand ye gazing up into heaven? this same Jesus which is taken up from you into heaven shall so come in like manner as ye have seen Him go into heaven." (Acts 1: 11.) In like manner—surely this does not mean a *spiritual* coming. If it means a spiritual coming, one might just as well say His ascension did not really take place. We have to look at it as spiritual, or, as some say, allegorical. No —in like manner means His visible and glorious return. The cloud took Him up, the cloud brings Him back. Jewish disciples (*not the church, for there was no church* when our Lord went back to

113

Heaven) saw Him returning to the glory; Jewish disciples will see Him coming back in like manner. He left the earth from the Mount of Olives; He returns to the earth to the Mount of Olives. (Zech. 14:5.)

The conversion of Saul of Tarsus (Acts 9) is also giving us lessons concerning the return of the Lord. Paul in his Epistle speaks of it as a pattern. It is the pattern of Israel's future national conversion. Saul saw the heavens opened,* and He saw Jesus and heard His voice. The light which he saw was above the brightness of the sun (Acts 26:13). The sun paled before that light of Him who is the Sun of Righteousness. Like Saul of Tarsus, Israel will see His glory and hear His voice. The many other passages we do not mention here, but refer to but one more in the book of Revelation, where His return in power and glory is described:

"And I saw heaven opened, and behold, a white horse, and one sitting on it called Faithful and True, and He judges and makes war in righteousness. And His eyes are a flame of fire, and upon His head many diadems, having a name written which no one knows but Himself; and He is clothed with a garment dipped in blood; and His name is called The Word of God. And the armies which are in the

*Three manifestations of the glorified Christ are given in the New Testament. He appeared unto Stephen, who saw Him standing (Acts 7.) Then to Saul on the road of Damascus, and the last to John in Patmos. Thus He will appear to His own, represented by Stephen, to receive them, to Israel and to the world, as seen in Revelation.

114

heaven followed Him upon white horses, clad in white, pure fine linen. And out of His mouth goes a sharp two-edged sword, that with it He smite the nations; and He shall shepherd them with an iron rod: and He treads the winepress of the fury of the wrath of God the Almighty. And he has upon His garment and upon his thigh a name written, King of kings and Lord of lords." (Rev. 19: 11-16.)

It is all in fullest accord with the witness of the Spirit in the Old Testament.

In conclusion we wish to remark that the coming of the Lord, the blessed Hope of the church, is something entirely different from the visible and glorious manifestation of the Lord. The blessed Hope is our gathering together unto Him. (2 Thess. 2: 1.) Such a Hope is not revealed in the Old Testament, for the church was then unrevealed. This blessed Hope means that the complete Body of Christ, the saints who have fallen asleep and the saints who are alive, shall be caught up together in clouds to meet the Lord in *the air*. No one knows when this Body may be complete, therefore this Hope is an imminent Hope. He may come for His own *to-day*. Gathered there in the air with Him, seeing Him as He is, we will appear before Him at His judgment seat, and sit down at the marriage supper, while in the earth the scenes of tribulation and judgments go on. When at last the moment comes of Jehovah's visible and glorious manifestation over the earth and coming down into the earth, the manifestation of the church will follow, for she is His bride. " When Christ our life is manifested, we will be manifested with Him in glory." He as Son brings many sons to glory. No eyes of such who are believers now saved by grace will see Him coming in the clouds, for they shall be with Him when He appears. Well may we earnestly pray, " Even so, come, Lord Jesus," the prayer to take us unto Himself.

VII

THE CONVERSION AND RESTORATION OF ISRAEL

WE begin now to look at the blessed things which are connected with the manifestation of Jehovah, our Lord Jesus Christ. From the preceding chapters we have learned that His appearing will be in the day, which is called " the day of the Lord," that this day will come at the end of the great tribulation, during which the nations form ungodly alliances to oppose God and His Anointed, and that Jehovah's manifestation will bring their judgment. But while that day is a day of wrath, it is also a day in which Jehovah will show mercy and fulfil all that which He spoke through the mouth of His holy prophets. A new age will begin, the age long foretold, when righteousness and peace kiss each other, when the nations learn war no more, and the knowledge of the glory of the Lord will cover the earth as the waters cover the deep.

We shall look first of all to the Harmony of all Prophecy in predicting the conversion and restoration of Israel. This topic is one of the most prominent in the prophetic Word. We find it quite a task in the limited space we have to condense all in such a way that the reader will get the correct, scriptural view of it, and to show at the same time how the Spirit of God bears witness to this great future of Israel.

It may not be altogether out of place to say whom we mean by Israel. There is so much wrong teaching about, that one is forced to refer almost constantly to the most simple foundation truths. The fact is that the most popular interpretation of the Bible makes Israel mean the church. Thus it has come to pass that all these wonderful prophecies which speak of a restoration of Israel and the blessings in store for them have been claimed to mean the " spiritual Israel," the church, and that this present age sees the fulfilment of these promises. This is totally wrong. This method of spiritualizing promises which relate exclusively to one people and one land has thoroughly carnalized the church. When God says Israel He means Israel and not the church. When God reveals the mystery hid in former ages, unknown in the Old Testament, the mystery of the church or assembly and His gracious purposes concerning this body, He does not mean Israel. So let us understand that Israel *is* Israel, namely, the descendants of Abraham, God's ancient people, the earthly people of God. When we speak therefore of the restoration of Israel, and cite from the Scriptures prophecy after prophecy, we mean that which God the Holy Spirit meant, the literal fulfilment of all these prophecies in the literal Israel to whom their own prophets transmitted these oracles of God.

It has been our privilege to witness during the past twenty years to thousands of believers concerning God's faithfulness towards Israel and their glorious future, and many have told us and more have written that the right key for the Bible was put into their hands when they saw Israel means Israel and not the church, when they understood God's loving purpose concerning that people whom He, in His sovereign mercy, chose to be His people. And so it is. If we begin to divide the Word of Truth rightly concerning the Jews, the Gentiles, and the church of God, and see that God has His plan clearly outlined in His Word for each of the three, and has fully revealed that when He began to take out of the nations a people for His name, the gathering of the church, He has not completely and finally cast away His earthly people Israel, we shall then surely have the right key which opens up all in God's Word. But this key has been lost by Christendom. If it were in the possession of the Higher Critics they could no longer sit in judgment upon the infallible Word of God, and all the present-day confusion of a professing church *trying* to attend to the calling and work of Israel in a future age, and worse than failing in it, dishonouring God and the Master who bought them, this confusion could no longer exist if it were understood God means Israel and that there is a restoration of Israel coming which places that people at the head of the nations, who will be brought to the knowledge of the Glory of the Lord by that restored people.

Now, perhaps the best way to approach this subject is by turning first to the Epistle to the Romans. In this Epistle the salvation in Christ is unfolded, which is for him who believes. This salvation is for the believing Jew and the believing Gentile, who are seen in the first part of the Epistle as guilty before God. With the 4th chapter the Jew, so to speak, is left out of sight, and we read only of what God has done for us in the gift of His Son and the place He gives in Him to every believing sinner. After this is fully made known, ending in the 8th chapter and before the Spirit of God speaks of the walk of the one who is in Christ, the Holy Spirit inserts three chapters, the 9th, 10th, and 11th, in which He makes dispensational facts prominent. He shows that God, in His dealings with the nations or with the Jews, is not unrighteous, and especially does He prove that the temporary rejection of Israel is not a complete rejection, nor is it final and permanent. And why this in Romans? We can well imagine the Jew stepping up after reading and hearing of a salvation in which Jews and Gentiles are treated alike, saying, " What about the promises made to my fathers? What about our peculiar place God in His sovereignty has given to us, and the hundreds of unfulfilled promises which were given to us through the prophets?" To tell the inquiring Jew that God didn't mean exactly the Jews when He gave these promises, that God had the church in mind, and that now He is through with the seed of Abraham and Abraham's land, would never satisfy him, he would and certainly could then accuse God of being unrighteous in breaking the oath-bound covenants made with the fathers. This is the reason why the Spirit of God puts into Romans this parenthesis of three chapters. And the fact that God *is* faithful to Israel, that He has not cast away His people Israel, that His gifts and callings are without repentance, is of great importance to us as believers of the Gentiles. Supposing it were so, as it is so generally claimed, that God is done with the seed of Abraham and that what He said through the prophets about Israel He meant for the church; what assurance could we have that God would be faithful to His promises made to us and do what He said? Who could guarantee us then against the possibility that God doesn't exactly mean what He promises about the church now and in a future age. May He not drop those He took out of the nations and saved in Christ, as He dropped Israel? How comforting, then, the fact that God's gifts and calling are without repentance. And this is shown about Israel in these chapters. In the 9th chapter of Romans we are told that to Israel *belongs* the adoption, the glory, the covenants and the law giving, and the service and the

promises, but it is in the 11th chapter in which
the Holy Spirit asks the question: "Hath God
cast away His people?" and in which so emphatically He says "Far be the thought!" and gives
His own answer to that question, proving that Israel
is Israel still, and what God promised to them He
is going to keep. That chapter must be studied in
detail to be fully understood. First, Paul is mentioned as an argument that God has not cast away
His people. In him, his conversion and his life,
God gave a sample and a type of what He can do
and will do with Israel, as unbelieving, fanatical,
and zealous without knowledge as Saul of Tarsus
was. Then He refers us to the fact that there was
never a time in the history of Israel when in their
greatest apostasy God had not reserved a remnant
for Himself. Elijah's time is used as an illustration. Though he complained of a universal
apostasy, God had seven thousand and knew them
who had not bowed the knee to Baal. Even so
now God has a remnant according to the election
of Grace. Answer upon answer follows in this
chapter showing God's purpose towards Israel and
their final conversion and restoration as a nation.
There is the illustration of the good olive tree and
the wild olive tree, and then the mystery is made
known so that the Gentile believer should not be
wise in his own conceits. "For I do not wish you
to be ignorant, brethren, of this mystery, that ye
may not be wise in your own conceits, that blind-

ness in part has happened to Israel, *until* the fulness of the Gentiles has come in, and so all Israel shall be saved, according as it is written, The deliverer shall come out of Sion; He shall turn away ungodliness from Jacob. And this is the covenant from me to them, when I shall take away their sins." (Rom. 11:25, 26.)

Alas! Christendom has been and is wise in their own conceits and is boasting against the broken-off branches. Christendom heeds not the warning " Be not highminded but fear: if God, indeed, spared not the natural branches, lest it might be He spared not thee either." Even these most simple statements about Israel and their final conversion in Romans 11 have been taken to mean the church. This is as bad as a person who came to us last year after having spoken on the verse " Jerusalem shall be trodden down by the Gentiles until the times of the Gentiles shall be fulfilled." After showing Jerusalem's future the person said, " But God can't mean the Jerusalem in Palestine; He means the Jerusalem *above*." This is a fair example of what some of the commentators have done and what some of the modern preachers do with the declarations of God's holy prophets. If they read of Jerusalem trodden down by the Gentiles—the Jews punished for their sins and unbelief, their land taken from them, and they scattered among the nations—of course it must mean Jerusalem and the Jews. But when the same verse says

Jerusalem shall not be trodden down by the Gentiles forever, Jerusalem shall become the city of a great King, the dispersed of Israel shall be gathered and brought back, etc., then we are told "it can't mean this same Jerusalem, we must apply this to the church, there is nothing left for the Jew." Oh, the blindness, unbelief, and arrogant pride of professing Christendom in rejecting God's purposes. We have thus briefly indicated that the subject before us, which is so fully revealed in the prophetic Word, the conversion and restoration of Israel, is a very pronounced New Testament doctrine and is a part of the faith once and for all delivered to the Saints.

We shall now turn our attention to the Old Testament Scriptures.

In the prophecy of Noah, Shem stands out prominently, and his supremacy is there indicated. (Genesis 9:25-29.) Later God called out of Shem one man, Abraham, and He made to him unconditional and absolute promises. "The God of Glory appeared unto our father Abraham" (Acts 7:2), said Stephen in beginning his testimony to the national leaders.

"And Jehovah said to Abram, Go out of thy land, and from thy kindred, and from thy father's house, to the land that I will show thee: and I will make of thee a great nation, and bless thee, and make thy name great: and thou shalt be a blessing: and I will bless them that bless thee and curse him that curseth thee; and in thee shall all the families of the earth be blessed." (Gen. 12:1-3.)

"And Jehovah appeared to Abram and said, Unto thy seed will I give this land" (Gen. 12:7).

"And Jehovah said to Abram, after that Lot hath separated himself from him, Lift up thine eyes, and look from the place where thou art northward, and southward, and eastward, and westward: for all the land that thou seest will I give to *thee* and to *thy seed for ever.* And I will make thy seed as the dust of the earth, so that if any one can number the dust of the earth, thy seed also will be numbered. Arise, walk through the land, according to the length of it and according to the breadth of it; for I will give it to thee" (Gen. 13:14-17).

"On the same day Jehovah made a covenant with Abram, saying, Unto they seed I give this land, from the river of Egypt to the great river, the river Euphrates" (Gen. 15:18).

These and similar promises made to Abraham, Isaac, and Jacob are the germs of all which the prophetic Word has to say of Israel's future restoration. A very little of what God promised unconditionally to Abraham has been fulfilled. He never possessed the land, nor did his seed possess it in the dimensions as promised to Abraham in the above passage. God came to Jacob and in the vision at night He said to him:

"I am Jehovah, the God of Abraham thy father, and the God of Isaac: the land on which thou liest, to thee will I give it and to thy seed. And thy seed shall be as the dust of the earth, and thou shalt spread abroad to the west, and to the east, and to the north, and to the south; and in thee and in thy seed shall all the families of the earth be blessed. And behold I am with thee and will keep thee in all places to which thou goest, and will bring thee again into this land; for *I will not leave thee until I have done* what I have spoken to thee of." (Gen. 28:13-15.)

The wanderer proceeded, and away from the land which was his by God's free gift, he suffers and sees evil days, yet God keeps what He said, never leaves him, and brings him back to the land. As He did to Jacob so does He to Jacob's seed. He will surely do all He has promised them and bring them back to their land. The fact that Jehovah does it, that it is His hand that accomplishes it all, is seen everywhere in the prophetic Word. *"I will"* is the word of Hope for Israel.

It would take many, many pages to follow all which is revealed in the Word concerning Israel's future and to trace the ever-increasing expansion of the promises made to the fathers of the nation. So we have to pass by much and cannot take up prophecies such as Jacob's in Genesis 49, in which the events are predicted which will befall the sons of Jacob in the *last days.* We confine ourselves to only a few of the large numbers of prophecies. If we turn once more to the utterances of Balaam, the man who came to curse Israel and was used by the Spirit of God to declare the blessedness of God's people, we shall find much which relates to this topic:

"Lo, it is a people that shall dwell alone, and not be reckoned among the nations. Who can count the dust of Jacob and the number of the fourth part of Israel?" (Num. 23:9-10.)

Israel is a separated people. The separation took place from the side of Jehovah. "I am the Lord your God, which have separated you from other people." "I have severed you that you should be mine." They are still a people dwelling alone and not reckoned among the nations. All the fires of persecution, inquisition, and tortures could not wipe them out, nor force them to abandon their peculiar and separated position. Assimilation with other nations, which is so much advanced by some of their own leaders, has failed likewise. Their separation and miraculous increase vouchsafe a future distinct work for them. Their separation and preservation is a Divine miracle.

Again, Balaam said:

"He hath not seen iniquity in Jacob, neither hath He seen wrong in Israel" (Num, 23:21).

This shows how God looks upon that people. They were sinful and are so now in their apostasy and unbelief. Yet God looks upon them in the light of His own marvellous Grace. They are a nation to be fully justified of all things—by God's sovereign Grace, as we as individuals are justified. Oh, let us not forget that important Word in the Gospel of John spoken by another one like Balaam, who had to declare a truth he did not know himself. Caiaphas, the high priest, prophesied and said that one man (our Lord) should die for the people, and that the whole nation perish not. And this spake he not of himself, but being a high priest that year, he prophesied that Jesus should *die for that nation.* (John 11:49-52.) Our Lord died for the nation, and on account of that precious blood that nation will be justified, and the day will come when it shall be true as God beholds them " no iniquity in Jacob, no wrong in Israel."

And once more we listen to Balaam's prophecy:

> "How goodly are thy tents, Jacob;
> And thy tabernacles, Israel!
> Like valleys are they spread forth,
> Like gardens by the river side,
> Like aloe trees which Jehovah has planted,
> Like cedars beside the waters.
> Water shall flow out of his buckets,
> And his seed shall be in great waters."
>
> (Num. 24:5-7.)

Here is a description of a future blessedness which is still to come and of which prophet after prophet speaks as moved by the Holy Spirit.

At the end of the book of Deuteronomy we read of the blessings and the curses which are in store for that people. The curses as they are enumerated in the 28th chapter have been literally fulfilled and are still being fulfilled in that nation. Centuries before it ever came to pass the Spirit of God outlines through Moses the history of the people whom he had led forth out of Egypt. Here is a fact which silences infidelity. As it has often been said, the Jew and his history of blood and tears and his *miraculous* preservation is the most powerful argument for the Divinity of the Bible. In the 30th chapter in Deuteronomy we

128

read something still more startling than the curses in the preceding chapters. Here we have a prophecy which foretells the future of Israel. It is still waiting for its fulfilment:

"And it shall come to pass when all these things are come upon thee, the blessing and the curse, which I have set before thee, and thou shalt take them to heart among all the nations whither Jehovah thy God has driven thee, and shalt return to Jehovah thy God, and shalt hearken to His voice according to all that I command thee this day, thou and thy sons, with all thy heart and all thy soul; that *then* Jehovah thy God will turn thy captivity and have compassion on thee, and will return and will gather thee from all the nations whither Jehovah thy God has scattered thee. Though there were of you driven out unto the ends of the heavens, from thence will Jehovah thy God gather thee, and from thence will He fetch thee; and Jehovah thy God will bring thee into the land that thy fathers possessed, and thou shalt possess it; and He will do thee good and multiply thee above thy fathers. And Jehovah thy God will circumcise thy heart, and the heart of thy seed, to love Jehovah thy God with all thy heart, and with all thy soul, that thou mayest live. And Jehovah thy God will put all these curses upon thine enemies, and on them that hate thee, who have persecuted thee. But thou shalt return and hearken unto the voice of Jehovah, and do all His commandments, which I command thee this day" (1-8).

Let us briefly notice the predictions and promises which are given in this passage.

First we notice the sentence, "Thou shalt take them to heart among *all the nations* whither Jehovah thy God has driven thee. This is a prophecy relating to the present dispersion of the Jews among all the nations. Some have said that this prophecy found its fulfilment when God sent the Jews into the Babylonian captivity and in the return of a small remnant. It will be seen by the first glance that it relates to another dispersion and to greater blessings than those which followed the restoration of the remnant of Jews who returned from Babylon. In the second place, the promise declares that their captivity among all the nations shall be turned and *Jehovah Himself will return.* This return of Jehovah means, as we find later in prophecy, the Second Coming of Christ, the glorious manifestation of Jehovah, as we described it in the preceding chapter. Thirdly, the passage predicts that after Jehovah returns they will be gathered from all the nations and be brought back to the land of their fathers, and there He will do them good. The circumcision of the heart is their conversion. Of all this, only their scattering among all the nations is accomplished, and all the rest is not yet. But He who scattered them will surely gather them. His Word is forever settled in the heavens.

We cannot very well pass by the 32d and 33d chapters of the same book. The 32d has been before us a number of times. While Moses here, through the Spirit of God, predicts the great apostasy of the people and the results " *scattered into the corners of the earth,*" he also predicts the end and the blessings for poor Israel. It is Jehovah who says in this song of Moses, " I kill and I make alive. I wound and I kill " (verse 39). It is His solemn pledge to Israel. He has slain them on account of their disobedience. Their death is spiritual and national. He will make them alive. They have been wounded, they shall be healed by Him. The last stanza of this song declares the happy future of the nations and of Israel in the coming age, which will be ushered in with the manifestation of Jehovah.

" Rejoice, oh ye nations, with his people [Israel] ; for He will avenge the blood of His servants and render vengeance to His adversaries, and will be merciful to His land and to His people " (verse 43). The 33d chapter gives the glorious state of all Israel in the coming age when they are converted and restored. Then it shall all be true what we read here:

> "There is none like unto the God of Jeshurun,
> Who rideth upon the heavens to thy help,
> And in His majesty upon the clouds.
> Thy refuge is the God of old,
> And underneath are the eternal arms;
> And He shall drive out the enemy from before thee,
> And shall say: Destroy them!
> And Israel shall dwell in safety alone,
> The fountain of Jacob, in a land of corn and new wine,
> Also His heavens shall drop down dew.
> Happy art thou, Israel!
> Who is like unto thee, a people saved by Jehovah,
> The shield of thy help,
> And the sword of thine excellency!
> And thine enemies shall come cringing to thee;
> And thou shalt tread upon their high places."
>
> (33 : 26-29.)

And what shall we select from scores of prophecies found in the Book of Psalms? Here, indeed, the blessedness which awaits God's ancient people after the long night of their suffering is fully described, and all in fullest harmony with the testimony of the prophets. We can take but a little from the rich revelation of this theme in the Psalms. "Oh that the salvation of Israel were come out of Zion! When Jehovah turneth again the captivity of His people, Jacob shall be glad, Israel shall rejoice." (Ps. 14:9.) This is one of the first passages in the Psalms relating to Israel's salvation. It is to come out of Zion, and the assurance is given that the captivity of His people *is* to be turned. Precisely that which God's Spirit declared through Moses. In our last chapter we quoted from the 29th Psalm, a judgment Psalm. If we turn to the last verse, we read what will happen after the voice of Jehovah has been heard upon the waters.

"Jehovah giveth strength to His people, Jehovah blesseth His people with peace."

It is after the manifestation of Himself that He blesses His people. The next Psalm, the 30th, continues this revelation, and in it we hear Israel's voice, restored and delivered, praising her Lord:

"Thou hast turned for me my mourning into dancing; thou hast loosed my sackcloth and girded me with gladness; that my glory may sing psalms of thee, and not be silent. Jehovah my God, I will praise thee forever."

Even so it shall be with God's people beloved
for the Father's sake. Their weeping endureth for
a night, but joy cometh in the morning. After
the 45th Psalm, which shows the coming of the
King, we find the next three Psalms revealing what
will be the result of this coming for the people who
rejected Him once. Israel knows Him now and
breaks forth in singing:

> "He subdueth the nations under us and the peoples under
> our feet. He hath chosen an inheritance for us, the excel-
> lency of Jacob, whom He loved." (Ps. 47:3, 4.)

Or if we turn to the 80th and 81st Psalms, we
find another prophecy.

In the 80th Psalm, Israel pleads for deliverance.

It is that turning with the heart unto Jehovah of
which Moses speaks in Deuteronomy 30.

The remnant of Israel says here: "How long
shall thine anger smoke against the prayers of Thy
people?" Three times they plead, "Turn us again,
O God! let thy face shine upon us and we shall be
saved." The ending of this Psalm is the most
significant.

> "Let thy hand be upon *the man of thy right hand,* upon
> the *Son of man* whom thou hast made strong for Thyself.
> So will we not go back from Thee. Revive us, and we will
> call upon Thy name. *Restore us,* O Jehovah, God of Hosts;
> cause Thy face to shine and we shall be saved."

The Son of Man, the Man at the right hand of
God, the Man raised from the dead and made

strong, is our Lord Jesus Christ, and He at last will be the restorer of Israel. So, then, in harmony with this we read in the next Psalm:

"Sing ye joyously unto God our strength, shout aloud unto the God of Jacob. Raise a song and sound the tambour, the pleasant harp with the lute."

The entire 103d Psalm stands dispensationally for the praise of restored Israel. So the 118th Psalm. It is the language of the converted nation:

"I will give thanks unto thee, for thou didst answer me.
Thou art become my salvation.
The Stone which the builders rejected
Hath become the head of the corner.
This is of Jehovah, it is wonderful in our eyes.

.   .   .   .

Blessed be He that cometh in the name of Jehovah."
(Ps. 118: 22, 23-26.)

Read Matthew 21:42-45 and Matthew 23:39. Here we have a chain of predictions which can only be literally fulfilled. He, our Lord, was the stone, and they rejected Him. His last word to them was that He would be hid from their eyes till they would say that word, " Blessed is He that cometh in the name of Jehovah." The 118th Psalm tells us that it will be so. What a harmony! How dare men reject the book of Psalms and declare that there is nothing about Christ in that book!

But we have to leave this wonderful collection of inspired songs, the last of which are rising higher and higher in praise and worship of Jehovah for

what He has done in earthly deliverances for His
people Israel.

From Joel, the seer of Jehovah's day, we quote
the following unfulfilled prophecies:

> " *Then* Jehovah will be jealous for His land and will
> have pity on His people. And Jehovah will answer and say
> unto His people, Behold, I send you corn, and new wine,
> and oil, and ye shall be satisfied therewith; and I will no
> more make you a reproach among the nations" (2: 18, 19).

The spiritual blessings are also promised to the
restored people in that day.

> "And it shall come to pass afterwards that I will pour
> out my Spirit upon all flesh; and your sons and your
> daughters shall prophesy; your old men shall dream dreams;
> your young men shall see visions. Yea, even upon the
> bondmen and upon the handmaids in those days will I pour
> out my Spirit" (2: 28, 29).

It will be seen from this prophecy that the fulfilment of this passage falls into the time of Israel's
restoration. Persons who apply it to the present
age make havoc of God's purposes and often drift
into fanciful teachings or even delusions.

At the close of the prophet Amos we have a
very simple prophecy, one which has special interest
because the Holy Spirit quotes it in the beginning
of the Christian age:

> "In that day will I raise up the tabernacle of David
> which is fallen down, and close up the breaches thereof;
> and I will raise up its ruins, and I will build it as in the

days of old: that they may possess the remnant of Edom, and all the nations upon whom my name is called, saith Jehovah who doeth this" (Amos 9: 11, 12).

It is in Acts 15: 13-18, where the Holy Spirit lifts this, His own prediction, into prominence. There He unfolds the divine programme of the ages.

1. He takes out a people for His name; which is the formation of the body, the church, still going on.

2. He returns. His coming again.

3. He rebuilds the tabernacle of David, etc. The restoration of Israel.

4. The residue of men, *after* Israel's restoration seek the Lord, which is world conversion.

How simple it is to comprehend and understand it!

But the last verse of Amos has a still greater significance. Will not our brethren who spiritualize all these predictions or who put their fulfilment in the past event of a returning remnant of Jews from the Babylonian captivity look carefully at this verse?

"And I will plant them upon their land, and they shall *no more* be plucked up out of their land which I have given them, saith Jehovah thy God" (9: 15).

Now, it is evident God speaks here concerning the people who were plucked up out of their land. The "church" was never plucked out of a land. It is Israel. He promises to plant them into their land again, and assures them that they shall NO MORE be plucked out of that land. There is then a double possibility: either this Word was fulfilled (as it is claimed) in the return of a Jewish remnant from Babylon, or it was not, and then it *must* be fulfilled in the future. It was not fulfilled in the return of the remnant, because that remnant *was* plucked out of the land. Therefore, every believer who believeth that God spake all these words *must* believe in a future restoration of Israel.

Hosea gives us additional proofs. Read chapter 2 : 14-23, and find there one of the many striking and plain predictions of the restoration of that people who for a time were " Lo Ammi," not my people. In the 3d chapter we read the passage which hardly can be spiritualized:

> " For the children of Israel shall abide many days without a king, and without a prince, and without a sacrifice, and without an image, and without an ephod and teraphim. Afterwards shall the children of Israel *return* and seek the Lord their God, and David their king; and shall fear the Lord and His goodness in the latter days" (3:4, 5).

They are now in the condition as described in the 4th verse, and they shall by-and-bye return and be converted as a nation.

Still other passages are in chapter 6 : 1-3, the confession of the nation in turning to Jehovah. Notice how they plead. It is in the language of Moses' prophetic Song (Deut. 32 : 39.) Wonderful, is it not? And they tell us there is nothing in prophecy, no harmony, and no intelligence!

The entire 14th chapter of Hosea shows the coming conversion and restoration of Israel.

To quote all which the Spirit of God reveals in the prophet Isaiah about Israel's conversion and future restoration, as well as the glory promised to them, would take many pages. Isaiah has been called "the Evangelical Prophet"; he might be called also "the Prophet of Israel's deliverance and glory." The scope of the book shows the aim of the Holy Spirit to reveal through past events and past deliverances of the nation the still greater events connected with Israel's restoration. If we turn to the 11th chapter we find there one of the most simple and unanswerable predictions of the restoration of Israel. The 10th chapter describes the advance of the Assyrian and his downfall, typical as we have seen before of the final Assyrian. The coming of Jehovah is seen in the beginning of the 11th. He comes to judge in righteousness, and with the breath of His mouth He slays the wicked. Then follow the blessed results, such as Deliverance of groaning creation, Peace on earth, and the restoration of Israel,

"And it shall come to pass in *that day,* that the Lord shall set His hand again the second time to recover the remnant of His people, which shall be left, from Assyria, and from Egypt, and from Pathros, and from Cush, and from Elam, and from Shinar, and from Hamath, and from the islands of the sea. And He shall lift up a banner to the nations, and shall assemble the outcasts of Israel and gather together the dispersed of Judah from the four corners of the earth" (11:11, 12).

It is strange that even such a plain prediction has been spiritualized or explained that it all happened long ago by the return of some 45,000 Jews from Babylon. This latter statement is easily disproved. The passage declares that " it shall come to pass in that day "—which is the day of Jehovah's visible manifestation. Furthermore, it is said that the Lord shall set His hand *again the second time* to recover the remnant of His people. It is then clearly stated that it is a *second* recovering. Besides this, we read that the recovery takes place of those who are in Assyria, and also from the islands of the sea. Now, in the Babylonian captivity none were brought back from the distant islands of the sea. Let us also notice that the outcasts of *Israel* will be assembled then, and the dispersed of *Judah* gathered. Those who returned from the Babylonian captivity were only Jews. Israel and Judah will be regathered and reunited in that day. It is a vain speculation to try and find the so-called ten lost tribes now. The Anglo-Israel theory is unscriptural and a delusion. The Lord knows where the whole house of Israel and the house of Judah is, and He will bring them all back.

The 12th chapter of Isaiah is the record of the song of praise which God's restored earthly people will sing. The 13th chapter predicts the downfall and judgment of Babylon, and in the beginning of the 14th we read what is closely connected with the judgment which falls at last upon the enemies of God's people.

"For Jehovah will have mercy on Jacob, and will yet choose Israel, and set them in rest in *their own land;* and the stranger shall be united to them and they shall be joined to the house of Jacob. And the peoples shall take them and bring them to their place; and the house of Israel shall possess them in the *land of Jehovah* for servants and handmaids, and they shall take them captive whose captives they were, and they shall rule over their oppressors" (14: 1, 2).

In the midst of the chapters to which we referred before, Isaiah's little Apocalypse, we read the following:

"In *that day* shall this song be sung in the land of Judah: We have a strong city: salvation does He appoint for walls and bulwarks. Open ye the gates and the righteous nation which keepeth faithfulness shall enter in. Thou wilt keep in perfect peace the mind stayed on thee, for He confideth in thee. Confide ye in Jehovah for ever, for in Jah, Jehovah, is the rock of ages. For He bringeth down them that dwell on high; the lofty city He layeth low, He layeth it low to the ground, He bringeth it even to the dust" (26: 1-5).

This is the song which the redeemed seed of Abraham will sing in the land of Judah when once more Jehovah dwells with them.

In the 22d chapter we read another very striking prediction:

"Upon the land of my people shall come up thistles and briars, yea, upon all the houses of joy of the joyous city. For the palace shall be deserted, the multitude of the city shall be forsaken, hill and watch-towers shall be caves for ever, a joy of wild asses, a pasture of flocks" (verses 13, 14).

This, then, is judgment. It has been literally fulfilled. The land which flowed once with milk and honey has become one of thistles and briars. The joyous city is a joyless place now, and the palace of the king is deserted. But this is not all. We stopped in the middle of a sentence and we must read on and see what is said of the same land, city, and people who are in judgment now.

"Until the Spirit be poured upon us from on high, and the wilderness become a fruitful field, and the fruitful field be counted for a forest. And judgment shall inhabit the wilderness and the work of righteousness shall be peace; and the effect of righteousness, quietness, and assurance for ever. And my people shall dwell in a peaceable habitation and in sure dwellings, and in quiet resting places" (verses 15-19).

The present desolation of the land and Jerusalem will have an end. The Spirit from on high will be poured upon them, and with this great coming event the changes promised in the above passage will take place. Let none say the Spirit from on high *has been* poured out upon the land. The condition of the land of Israel and the palace proves that the Spirit has not been poured out in the full sense of the word. It is a promise in harmony with the one in Joel 2.

In the 33d chapter there is another comfortable word spoken, which will be realized in the future.

"Look upon Zion, the city of our solemnities; thine eyes shall see Jerusalem a quiet habitation, a tent that shall not be removed, the stakes whereof shall never be pulled up, neither shall any of its cords be broken; but there Jehovah is unto us glorious, a place of rivers, of broad streams, no galley with oars shall go there, nor shall gallant ships pass thereby" (verses 20, 21).

But what shall we quote from the second large section of Isaiah? Here indeed is prophecy upon prophecy which relates to Israel's conversion and restoration. The 1st chapter of the second part begins with the sublime assurance of the comfort of God for His people Israel.

"Comfort ye, comfort ye my people, saith your God. Speak to the heart of Jerusalem, and cry unto her, that her time of suffering is accomplished, that her iniquity is pardoned, for she hath received of Jehovah's hand double for all her sins" (40: 1, 2).

All through the chapters which follow there is a golden thread of comforting predictions relating to the topic before us. Israel restored and converted is seen as the servant of Jehovah, while in the 53d chapter the Messiah, the suffering One, is revealed. That chapter is much quoted and enjoyed by all believers, because it speaks of the blessed fact of the atonement made, the peace which was made in the blood of the cross; but we should not forget it has a deeper meaning. It is the repenting nation in the great national mourning to come, when Jehovah comes from Heaven, which will believingly say:

"Surely He hath borne our griefs and carried our sorrows, and we, we did not regard Him, stricken, smitten of God, and afflicted. But He was wounded for our transgressions, He was bruised for our iniquities, the chastisement of our peace was upon Him, and with His stripes we are healed. All we, like sheep, have gone astray, we have turned every one to his own way; and Jehovah has laid upon Him the iniquity of us all" (53:4-6).

The 54th chapter is one which is all occupied with the blessed results for Israel, after such a confession has come from their hearts and lips. What gracious promises! What assurances for their final blessings in the earth through the Mercy of God!

Then it will be that another gracious word given through Isaiah will be fulfilled. A word which will surely be fulfilled, when Israel looks upon Him whom they rejected.

"I have blotted out, as a thick cloud, thy transgressions, and, as a cloud, thy sins return unto Me, for I have redeemed thee. Sing, ye heavens, for Jehovah has done it; shout, ye lower parts of the earth; break forth into singing, ye mountains, the forest and every tree therein! For Jehovah has redeemed Jacob, and glorified Himself in Israel" (44:22, 23).

It is the actual manifestation of Israel's justification, as we heard it from Balaam's utterance. He has not beheld iniquity in Jacob. That which with the second coming of Christ, Israel's conversion, will take place is seen also from the 59th chapter.

"And the Redeemer will come to Zion, and unto them that turn from transgression in Jacob, saith Jehovah. And as for me this is my covenant with Him, saith Jehovah: My Spirit that is upon thee, and my words which I have put in thy mouth, shall not depart out of thy mouth, nor out of the mouth of thy seed, nor out of the mouth of thy seed's seed, saith Jehovah, from henceforth and for ever" (59: 20, 21).

Romans 11th, as we have seen, quotes the passage, and there the Spirit of God reveals the mystery that when the fulness of the Gentiles has come in all Israel shall be saved.

The three chapters which follow the 59th in Isaiah are chapters which acquaint us with the results of Jehovah's manifestation for the deliverance and salvation of Israel. What chapters these are, the 60th, 61st, and 62d! The spiritualizing of these chapters is the almost universal way in which they have been treated. We must leave this prophet and see how the Spirit of God speaks of the same event in the prophet Jeremiah.

Here we have numerous prophecies which, if closely examined, can mean nothing else but a literal restoration of Israel. Jeremiah 3: 12-19, is one of the first predictions in that prophet.

In the 16th chapter we find the following interesting passage:

"Therefore, behold the days come, saith Jehovah, that

it shall no more be said, As Jehovah liveth, who brought up the children of Israel out of the land of Egypt; but as Jehovah liveth, who brought up the children of Israel from the land of the north, and from all the lands whither He had driven them. For I will bring them again into their land, which I gave to their fathers" (16: 14, 15).

The great deed of Jehovah in taking His people out of Egypt is not only a type of the spiritual salvation which it so completely foreshadows, but it is also typical of the great coming, national conversion and restoration of Israel. The former shall be forgotten because Jehovah has stretched out His arm and brought His children back from the land of the north and from all the lands whither He had driven them. The Jew in dispersion now still looks back to the deliverance out of Egypt. He keeps the memorial of that great event, the Passover, the feast of unleavened bread. Longingly he prays every year, " This year here, next year in Jerusalem; this year servants, next year free." He will not be disappointed in his hope and expectation, and when at last he is brought back he shall substitute the phrase, " as Jehovah liveth who brought up the children of Israel from the land of the north," for the phrase, " as Jehovah liveth, who brought the children of Israel out of the land of Egypt."

In the 23d chapter 5-8 is another prophecy which plainly foretells their literal restoration and the establishment of the theocracy in their midst. As we consider the theocratic kingdom in our next chapter, we shall pass this passage by.

But there are other prophecies in Jeremiah which relate to Israel's conversion and return to the land.

"Thus speaketh Jehovah the God of Israel, saying, Write thee in a book all the words that I have spoken unto thee. For behold, the days come, saith Jehovah, when I will turn the captivity of my people Israel and Judah, saith Jehovah; and I will cause thee to return to the land that I gave to their fathers, and they shall possess it" (30:2, 3).

That this word refers to the coming restoration is seen by the context which predicts in connection with it the time of Jacob's trouble. The same chapter contains other revelations of Israel's hope.

"And thou, my servant Jacob, fear not, saith Jehovah; neither be dismayed, O Israel; for behold, I will save thee from afar, and thy seed from the land of their captivity; and Jacob shall return and be in rest, and at ease, and none shall make him afraid. For I am with thee, saith Jehovah, to save thee: for I will make a full end of all the nations whither I have scattered thee; yet of thee will I not make a full end, but I will correct thee with judgment, and will not hold thee altogether guiltless" (30: 10-12).

The whole 31st chapter is one continued message of comfort and peace for Jerusalem. Their return and joyous singing is vividly described. The Word of Jehovah is also addressed to the nations. "Hear the Word of Jehovah, ye nations, and declare it to the isles afar off and say, He that scattered Israel will gather him and keep him as a shepherd his flock" (verse 10). This is followed in the chapter by the prophecy that a new covenant shall be established, and what blessing will be theirs as a nation in that covenant.

"I will put my law in their inward parts, and will write it in their hearts; and I will be their God and they shall be my people. And they shall teach no more any man his neighbour, and every man his brother, saying, Know Jehovah; for they shall all know me, from the least of these unto the greatest of them, saith Jehovah; for I will pardon their iniquity, and their sin I will remember no more" (verses 33, 34).

This is their national conversion. It is ridiculous to claim a past fulfilment of this prediction. Still it has been done, and it has been said that the remnant of Jews returning from Babylon had forgiveness of sin, and now the Jews have ceased to be a nation forever. The Holy Spirit evidently anticipated such a denial as well as the almost universal teaching of Christendom that the seed of Abraham is no longer a nation and has no national hope and national future. Therefore He adds the following:

"Thus saith Jehovah, who giveth the sun for a light by day, the ordinances of the moon and of the stars for a light by night, who stirreth up the sea, so that the waves thereof roar, Jehovah of Hosts is His name; if those ordinances depart from before me, saith Jehovah, the seed of Israel also shall cease from being a nation from before me for ever. Thus saith Jehovah: If the heavens above can be measured and the foundations of the earth be searched out beneath, I will also cast off the whole seed of Israel, for all that they have done, saith Jehovah" (verses 35-37).

The sun still shines and the moon still sends forth her given light, the waves still roar, the heights of

147

the heavens and the foundations of the earth are still unmeasured and unsearched, therefore Israel's end as a nation has not yet come. And all this is not the word of man; it is the Word of Jehovah, for we read twenty times in this chapter, " *Thus saith Jehovah.*"

But we have to see what other prophets declare. From Ezekiel we take but a few of the many passages. The 16th chapter is one of the largest in that prophet. It begins with relating what Jehovah had done for Jerusalem, how His mercy had lifted her up, and it shows the fall of the nation, their terrible apostasy, but at the close of the long rehearsal of his misery Jehovah assures her of His mercies towards her. He is the God who changeth not. " And I will establish my covenant with thee, and thou shalt know that I am Jehovah; that thou mayest remember, and be ashamed, and no more open thy mouth because of thy confusion when I forgive thee *all* thou hast done, saith the Lord Jehovah."

In the 34th chapter Jehovah reveals Himself as the Shepherd of Israel. He Himself will gather the lost sheep of the house of Israel and bring them back to their land.

"And they shall no more be a prey to the nations, neither shall the beasts of the earth devour them; but they shall dwell in safety and none shall make them afraid" (34:28).

The entire 36th chapter is Israel's comfort. It

is in the closest connection with the 30th chapter of Deuteronomy. There the Lord said what He will do, and here His Spirit repeats this assurance.

"Therefore say unto the house of Israel, Thus saith the Lord Jehovah: I do not this for your sakes, O house of Israel, but for my holy name, which ye have profaned among the nations whither ye went. And I will hallow my great name, which was profaned among the nations, which have profaned in the midst of them; and the nations shall know that I am Jehovah, saith the Lord Jehovah, when I shall be hallowed in you before their eyes. And I will take you from among the nations, and gather you out of all countries and will bring you into your own land. And I will sprinkle clean water upon you, and ye shall be clean: from all your uncleanness and from all your idols will I cleanse you. And I will give you a new heart, and I will put a new spirit within you; and I will take away the stony heart out of your flesh and I will give you a heart of flesh. And I will put my Spirit within you, and cause you to walk in my statutes and keep mine ordinances, and ye shall do them. And ye shall dwell in the land that I gave to your fathers, and ye shall be my people and I will be your God" (36: 24-31, and to the end of the chapter).

All this has been and is spiritually applied, and Israel has been robbed of her comfort and coming glory. The same has been done with the vision of the dry bones, which follows in the 37th chapter. The 11th verse makes clear what the Lord means with the vision:

"And he said unto me, Son of man, these bones are the whole house of Israel. Behold they say our bones are dried, and our hope is lost; we are cut off! Therefore prophesy and say unto them, Thus saith the Lord Jehovah: Behold I will open your graves, and cause you to come up out of your graves, O my people, and bring you into the land of Israel."

In the same chapter we read the prophecy of the coming union of both houses, the house of Judah and the house of Israel. Till then the ten tribes are hid, but in that day the children of Israel will be brought together out of the nations.

Another passage we quote from the 39th chapter:

"And they shall know that I am Jehovah, their God, in that I caused them to be led into captivity among the nations, and have gathered them unto their own land, and I leave *none* of them any more there. And I will not hide my face any more from them, for I shall have poured out my Spirit upon the house of Israel, saith the Lord Jehovah" (verses 28, 29).

These verses cannot be fulfilled because they are not yet in the land. Therefore they must be brought there in the future never to be under the displeasure of God again. The Spirit of Jehovah will then be poured out upon them. This is in perfect agreement with what we learned from Joel 2 and Isaiah 32. In Joel the Spirit is seen poured out after the Northern army is removed. In Ezekiel the same statement is made after the invasion of Gog and Magog from the north. Such is the harmony of God's prophets.

The end of Ezekiel describes the wonderful temple which will stand once more in Jerusalem, and that the very name of the city shall be changed to " Jehovah Shammah," Jehovah is there. Of this more in the chapters which follow. Daniel's prophecy concerns mostly the Gentile nations, yet he also indicates the fact of Israel's restoration and their final deliverance.

The whole episode from the life of the prophet Jonah as contained in the book which he wrote typifies Israel's disobedience, Israel's temporary rejection, and Israel's restoration. Jonah is a type of Israel, besides being a type of Christ. The whole history of the seed of Abraham, past, present, and future, is contained in a nutshell in that book.

Jonah's call. He is sent by Jehovah to preach to Nineveh. He knows God while Nineveh is in darkness. So God prepared Himself Israel a nation to show forth His praises. Salvation is of the Jews. Through them He desires to make known His loving kindness and His redemption. In the seed of Abraham all the nations of the earth are to receive blessing. These are God's gifts and calling. They are without repentance (Rom. 11 : 29).

Jonah is disobedient. He turns his back upon God and flees from His face. He goes on board of a merchantman. He goes in the opposite direction. So Israel became an apostate people, and the Jew turns merchant. They forsook God and lightly esteemed the rock of his salvation. Like Jonah, disobedient to the heavenly vision, instead of being a blessing they became a curse among the nations.

Trouble soon comes upon Jonah, the disobedient servant of God. The storm of disaster tosses his ship upon the wild waves of the angry sea. Everything is against him because he rebelled against God. Thus with the Jews. Misfortune after misfortune, storm after storm, has broken over them since they rejected God and their King Messiah. They are tossed about by the nations. The sea always represents nations in the Word.

Jonah does not deny his God and his nationality. He said, "I am a Hebrew and I fear the Lord, the God of Heaven, which has made the sea and the dry land." So the Jew in his apostasy still professes to be a believer in God, fears His name, and does not deny that he is a Jew.

Jonah is cast overboard. He is given up to the angry waves. He is seen struggling in the waves. Typical of the Jew being cast away, though not forever.

The men in Jonah's ship when they saw that as soon as Jonah was in the water the waters calmed down, these men, who were all heathen, feared the Lord exceedingly, and offered a sacrifice unto the Lord and made vows. What a wonderful illustration of the very statement in the Epistle to the Romans, chapter 11:11: "By their fall salvation has come to the Gentiles." The Gentiles have received salvation when the Jew was set aside nationally.

Jonah is miraculously preserved in the belly of a

sea monster. (There is nothing in the Hebrew to show that it was a whale.) He is to have his abode there for three days and three nights. He does not lose his life and existence, but he is put into a grave and is there wonderfully preserved. The Jew is likewise in his grave among the nations, nationally dead, but still God keeps the Jew as He did Jonah. The Jew is God's standing miracle. No infidel can explain away the Jew and his miraculous existence.

Jonah was not digested by the fish. He remained there undigested. The nations have not digested the Jews. This people shall dwell alone and not be reckoned among the nations. The Jew is still a Jew. Assimilation has failed.

Jonah at the end of the appointed time commenced to repent in his grave. He cried to God. He wished himself back to His holy temple, and he finished his prayer with the believing shout, " Salvation is of the Lord." The Jews will also repent. There are unmistakable signs of a changed attitude of the Jew noticeable. Still, before that great national repentance comes, there will be likewise first a great tribulation. Like Jonah, many are to-day desiring for His holy temple, and they are getting ready to return to the land. At last they will acknowledge that salvation is of the Lord, and welcome their King with the shout, " Blessed is He that cometh in the name of the Lord."

God made the fish vomit out Jonah. He that scattered Israel will gather them again. They will be brought back to the land and restored. They will build the waste places, the desolations of many generations.

Jonah is sent the second time, and he follows the command. So Israel is yet to fulfil its grandest mission. Their King, our coming Lord, will com-mission them again and send them forth to proclaim His salvation. Israel will then follow obediently.

The whole city of Nineveh repented after hearing the *apostate,* the *punished,* and the *restored* Jew preach. A whole city was swept by a revival. The masses were saved. Now is the time for the salvation of individuals. There is no such thing at this present time as saving the masses or converting the world. The masses will be saved and the world converted through the preaching of the Jews when they are converted and restored in the land and Jesus is crowned as their King and sits upon the throne of His Father David.

This, then, illustrates, at least in part and in a faint way, what their reception is and means, "Life from the dead" (Rom. 11:15).

From the rest of the prophets we give but a few quotations, in which the Holy Spirit gives the same witness concerning the future of Israel.

"I will surely assemble, O Jacob, the whole of thee; I will surely gather the remnant of Israel; I will put them together as the sheep of Bozrah, as a flock in the midst of pasture; they shall make great noise by reason of the multitude of men. One that breaketh through is gone up before them; they have broken forth, and have passed on to the gate, and are gone out of it; and their king passeth on before them, and Jehovah at the head of them" (Micah 2: 12, 13).

The 4th chapter in Micah also speaks of the restoration of Israel in the coming age, their blessedness and the kingdom established in their land. The 5th chapter continues this theme, and at the end of the prophet stands that sublime Word, which the orthodox Jew remembers from time to time and which shall find its fulfilment when at last the wanderings of the nation are over.

"Who is a God like unto thee, that forgiveth iniquity and passeth by the transgression of the remnant of the heritage? He retaineth not His anger for ever, because He delighteth in loving kindness. He will yet again have compassion upon us, He will tread under foot our iniquities; and thou wilt cast all their sins into the depths of the sea. Thou wilt perform truth to Jacob, loving kindness to Abraham, which thou hast sworn unto our fathers from the days of old" (Micah 7: 18-20).

Surely Israel will not be disappointed in her hope and expectation that the oath-bound promises made to Abraham, Isaac, and Jacob will ever fail.

Zephaniah 3 shows the restoration and conversion of Israel *after* the day of Jehovah, which is predicted and described in the 1st chapter.

"Sing, O daughter of Zion, shout, O Israel; rejoice and be glad with all thy heart, O daughter of Jerusalem: Jehovah has taken away thy judgments, He hath cast out thine enemy: the King of Israel, Jehovah, is in the midst of thee; thou shalt not see *evil any more*. . . . At that time will I bring you, yea, at the time that I gather you; for I will make you a name and a praise, among the peoples of the earth, when I shall turn again your captivity before your eyes, saith Jehovah" (Zeph. 3: 14-20).

In Zechariah's night visions and prophecies nearly all relates to the future of Israel. The first two night visions show what Jehovah will do to the Gentiles, and the third contains the vision of the restoration of Israel, the gathering of His people, and the manifestation of His glory (Zech. 2). The fourth night vision typifies under the cleansing of the high priest the cleansing of the nation, the high priest among the nations of the earth; and the fifth, the vision of the candlestick, is Israel cleansed and restored, the light for the Gentiles. The 8th chapter predicts directly the restoration of Jerusalem and her glory.

The conversion of the nation is vividly described in the 12th chapter.

"And I will pour upon the house of David and upon the inhabitants of Jerusalem the Spirit of grace and supplication; and they shall look at me whom they have pierced, and they shall mourn for Him, as one mourneth for an only son, and it shall be in bitterness for Him, as one that is in bitterness for His first-born . . . In *that day* there shall be a fountain opened to the house of David and to the inhabitants of Jerusalem for sin and for uncleanness" (12: 10-14; 13: 1).

This passage, besides being a confirmation of the witness contained in the other prophets of a coming outpouring of the Spirit, brings another interesting fact before us. It is Jehovah who speaks, and He speaks of Himself as pierced. What else does it mean than that He who comes and who appears before them is the One whom they rejected and delivered into the hands of the Gentiles, the One who speaks in the 22d Psalm, "They have pierced my hands and feet." When He comes the nail-prints in His hands and His feet will be visible to Israel. They were visible in His glorified body, and unbelieving Thomas, who put his fingers into them and cried out, "My Lord and my God," is a type of Israel. Unbelieving still, they will see Him at last as He is, and mourn for Him in a great national mourning. In the last chapter of Zechariah we see the nation delivered and restored.

The prophet Malachi closes this wonderful and harmonious testimony of Israel's restoration and conversion in that he says through the Spirit of God that " the Sun of Righteousness will arise with healing in His wings, and ye shall go forth and leap like fatted calves " (Mal. 4:2). The Sun of Righteousness is Jehovah in His visible manifestation.

Though we have devoted considerable space to this chapter, we have quoted only a few passages of the many which relate to Israel's future. However, enough has been given to show how great the harmony is which exists throughout the Word in the revelation of Israel's restoration and conversion.

It has also been shown when this will take place. It is closely connected with the manifestation of Jehovah. To deny this great core doctrine of the Old Testament is to reject the very Word of Jehovah.

In the beginning of this chapter we showed how prominent the future of Israel is made in the New Testament. There is absolutely nothing in the New Testament, no word from our Lord, nor in the witness of the Holy Spirit in the Epistles, which would authorize us to say this great theme of the Old Testament prophetic Word meant events in connection with a spiritual Israel.

In the next chapters we shall show restored Israel, her glory and work in the theocratic kingdom and throughout the coming age.

VIII

THE THEOCRATIC KINGDOM

A LITTLE while before our Lord Jesus Christ was taken up before the eyes of the assembled disciples, they asked Him, "Lord, wilt Thou at this time restore again the kingdom to Israel?" (Acts 1:6.) According to many interpreters of the Word these disciples were prompted to ask this question out of selfish motives and out of gross ignorance. It has been said they did not know any better. However, the Lord does not blame them, nor does He rebuke them, for asking this question. "And He said unto them, It is not for you to know the times or the seasons which the Father hath put in His own power." This answer is certainly an affirmation that the kingdom will be restored to Israel; only the times and seasons when it shall be are hid.

When our Lord came and began His ministry among His own He came to the lost sheep of the house of Israel. He preached the kingdom of the heavens at hand and demanded repentance. The same message was first preached by the forerunner, John the Baptist, and when the Lord sent forth His disciples with the command to preach "the kingdom of the heavens is at hand," He also gave them power to heal the sick, to cleanse the lepers, to raise the dead, and to drive out demons. The preaching of the kingdom was not received by the nation. The offer was rejected. First, the forerunner's message was rejected and he himself slain; then the Lord's offer was likewise rejected, which was followed by the rejection of the Lord, the King Himself.

Now the question is, What kingdom was it which our Lord offered to Israel? It was the kingdom which He promised to Israel in the Old Testament, a literal kingdom, which has for its seat Jerusalem; the throne of David established in it and upon this throne, ruling, a son of David. This kingdom is promised to extend from Jerusalem over the whole earth. This kingdom the Lord offered to Israel, and He Himself is the King and the rightful heir to the throne of David. This kingdom and their own King the Jewish people rejected. We are aware we are once more at issue with the greater part of Christendom. The generally accepted teaching is that John the Baptist and our Lord meant forgiveness of sins, conversion, the gift of the Holy Spirit, etc., by kingdom of the heavens, and of that promised literal kingdom nothing is said, or it is rejected. The outcome of ignoring the true meaning of the kingdom of the heavens in its relation to Israel and the earth, has been a deplorable confusion, a constant mixing up of promises which relate to the coming kingdom age, and to this present age. The simple gospel has also been affected by it, and there is in Christendom a continual talking of "building up the kingdom," and "working for the kingdom," and endeavours to bring "the masses into the kingdom," etc., which is unscriptural. The kingdom promised to Israel and their King was then rejected by the nation; however, this does not alter the fact that our Lord *is* the King of Israel, heir to the throne of David, and that this promised kingdom is His and will yet come in power and glory. It has not been abandoned by Israel's unbelief, but only *postponed*. Its coming is connected with the return of our Lord as Son of Man in glory. Christendom aims at having a kingdom without the king. The church is not that kingdom, nor could the church ever see a fulfilment of the earthly promises connected with the kingdom, for the church belongs to the heavenlies. Everything in its order. First: The King came and offered the kingdom, and they rejected both His kingdom and Himself. Second: The King comes again, and with His coming that kingdom once rejected will be established in the earth. Between this first coming of the King and His second coming is this present Christian age with its mysteries which were hidden in former ages. We only call attention in connection with these introductory remarks to this chapter to the fact that our Lord speaks of Himself as "the Son of Man coming in His Kingdom." He mentions His own throne upon which He will sit.

He speaks of Himself as One who has gone into a far country to receive a kingdom, and that He will return.

Still more striking is the Word of God, the Word of Divine appointment, as it was transmitted through Gabriel to Mary.

"And the angel said unto her, Fear not, Mary; for thou hast found favour with God. And behold, thou *shalt* conceive in thy womb, and bring forth a son, and thou *shalt* call His name Jesus. He *shall* be great and *shall* be called the Son of the Highest, and the Lord God *shall* give unto Him the throne of His father David; and He *shall* reign over the house of Jacob for ever, and of His kingdom there *shall* be no end" (Luke 1 : 30-33).

The little word " shall " we put in italics. It will be seen that it is found seven times in these three verses. Four of these divine " shalls " have been literally fulfilled; the other three await their literal fulfilment. The first four relate to the suffering of the Lord, to His humiliation, and the last three to His glory and His kingdom. As truly as Mary conceived in her womb by the Holy Spirit and brought forth a Son and His name was Jesus— He was great and called the Son of the Highest —just as truly will the other three unfulfilled " shalls " be fulfilled. He will receive the throne of his father David. He will reign over the house of Jacob and will possess a kingdom, which shall have no end. Well did the Spirit of God declare through Simeon, who held the child in his arms and who blessed the parents, for the child had no need of his blessing, " Mine eyes have seen thy salvation, which thou hast prepared before the face of all people; a light to lighten the Gentiles, and the glory of thy people Israel " (Luke 2 : 30-32). The glory of His people Israel is yet to come, and means the kingdom which will be set up in their midst by the Lord's return.

Now, throughout the Old Testament Scriptures we find prophecies upon prophecies which give us a complete description of this kingdom and Jerusalem, the glorious centre of it. We shall have to quote many passages which contain unfulfilled promises relating to this theocratic kingdom, its rule and the blessings through the same. In the course of these quotations we shall call the attention of the reader to some important facts concerning the rule *in* the earth and *over* the earth, the glory which is manifested in Jerusalem and the glory of the heavenly Jerusalem, the throne which stands in Jerusalem below and the glorious throne, which is in the heavenlies and visible from the earth. These distinctions have but little been recognized, and generally the church is placed in the earth during the kingdom age.

We remind the student of this volume briefly of the utterances of Balaam, which we considered before. Relating to the future and blessedness of the people he came to curse, we have in these several passages which speak of the King of Israel and His kingdom. " Jehovah his God is with him, and the shout of a King in his midst" (Numb. 23:21). "His King shall be higher than Agag, and His kingdom shall be exalted" (Numb. 24:7). "A Sceptre shall rise out of Israel, He shall cut in pieces the corners of Moab and destroy all the sons of tumult" (Numb. 24:17).

The Spirit of God declared through Balaam that Jehovah is with Israel. Jehovah Himself was the King of His people.

Up to Samuel, Israel had a theocratic rule. Then the elders of Israel gathered themselves together and came to Samuel at Ramah and said, "Now make us a king to judge us like all the nations." Futhermore we read:

"And Jehovah said unto Samuel, Hearken unto the voice of the people in all that they say unto thee, for they have not rejected thee, but they have rejected me, that *I should not reign over them.* According to all the works which they have done since the day that I brought them up out of Egypt even unto this day, wherewith they have forsaken me, and served other gods, so do they also unto thee. Now, therefore, hearken unto their voice, only testify solemnly unto them, and shew them the manner of king that shall reign over them" (1 Samuel 8:5-9).

Samuel then described the King they were going to have. Six times it is said of Him, "He will take." Yet in view of the dark picture the people said, "We will have a king over us." So they had rejected Jehovah their King and Jehovah gave them a King. The history which follows, the history of Saul and the history of David and his son Solomon, is extremely rich in its typical application. Israel under Saul is the type of Israel under the wicked king when Jehovah is rejected. David, of course, as shepherd-king, the man after the heart of God, is the type of our Lord. His sufferings and glories to which He comes through conquest are here richly foreshadowed. The Davidic reign typifies the beginning of that coming kingdom, when He who is the Son of David, according to the flesh, comes forth victoriously to subdue all His enemies and tread them under foot. Solomon, meaning peace, is the type of the Lord likewise. The Solomonic reign is the type of our Lord, Son of Man and King ruling the earth as Prince of Peace. Much as we would like we cannot enter into a closer study of these histories at this time. We shall, however, quote the words which form the basis of the Davidic covenant and which we find so often repeated in the prophets.

"And it came to pass that night that the Word of Jehovah came to Nathan, saying, Go and say unto my servant David, Thus saith Jehovah: Wilt thou build me a house for me to dwell in? For I have not dwelt in a house since the day that I brought up the children of Israel out of Egypt, even to this day, but I went about in a tent and in a tabernacle. In all my going about with all the children of Israel, did I speak a word with any of the tribes of Israel, whom I commanded to feed my people Israel, saying, Why build me not a house of cedars? And now, thus shalt thou say unto my servant David, Thus saith Jehovah of Hosts: I took thee from the pasture grounds, from following the sheep, to be prince over my people, over Israel; and I have been with thee whithersoever thou wentest, and I have cut off all thine enemies before thee, and have made thee a great name like unto the name of the great men that are in the earth. And I will appoint a place for my people, for Israel, and will plant them, that they may dwell in a place of their own, and be disturbed no more; neither shall the sons of wickedness afflict them any more, as formerly, and since the time that I commanded judges to be over my people Israel. And I have given thee rest from all thine enemies, and Jehovah tellest thee that Jehovah will make thee a house. When thy days are fulfilled, and thou shalt sleep with thy fathers, I will set up thy seed after thee, which shall proceed out of thy bowels, and I will establish his kingdom. It is he who shall build a house for my name, and I will establish the throne of his kingdom for ever. I will be his father and he shall be my son. If he commit iniquity I will chastise him with the rod of men and with the stripes of the sons of men; but my mercy shall not depart away from him, as I took it from Saul whom I put away from before me. And thy house and thy kingdom shall be made firm for ever before thee: thy throne shall be established for ever. According to all these words, and according to all this vision. So did Nathan speak to David" (2 Samuel 7:4-17).

David wanted to build a house for Jehovah; instead of that Jehovah tells him that He will build him a house. David praised Jehovah for these words of promise, trusting in every word the Lord had spoken through Nathan. That Solomon, the son of David, was partly in view is clear, but that this covenant Jehovah made with the house of David was not realized in Solomon and his reign is equally clear. The Messiah, the *Zemach* of David, Son of David, is here in full view, and in Him and through Him alone can this Davidic covenant be carried out. The Word in this passage, " I will be His Father and He shall be my Son," is quoted by the Holy Spirit in Hebrews 1 as referring to our Lord Jesus Christ. How harmonious it all is as we look at this covenant and then hear the message from God again, " He shall give Him the throne of His Father David" (Luke 1: 32). For this reason, to prove the legal title of Jesus Christ to the throne of David, do we find a genealogy the first thing in the gospel of Matthew, the royal gospel.

To David Jehovah made the promise, and He swore unto him that the throne of his kingdom is to be established forever, and one from his seed is to have this throne. In our Lord, the Son of David, according to the flesh, this oath-bound covenant will be kept and He will come forth as King of Israel and rule as such as well as King of kings and Lord of lords. Then the heavens are opened and He is manifested and comes back to earth once more, back to the Mount of Olives. He will assume the rule and receive His throne. However, it is here where we shall have to make some remarks which we trust will be helpful to a better understanding of the theocratic rule.

Not a few believers look upon the continued personal presence of our Lord as King, Son of David upon the throne of David, in the earth throughout the coming age as a scriptural fact. They look altogether to the earthly side, and believe the Lord must sit upon a throne in the earthly Jerusalem for a thousand years. They forget, however, that there is not only an earthly Jerusalem, but also a heavenly Jerusalem, and that the Lord is not only the King of Israel but also head of His body, which is the church. The abode of the church is with the Lord. The church will occupy His throne and rule and reign with Him over the earth. The place for the church, however, is not Jerusalem in the earth, but the heavenly Jerusalem. Nowhere is it said that the Lord and His body will be *in the earth* during the age which comes, when Israel's fulness has come. If the church is in the heavenly Jerusalem and not in the earth, then the Lord must be there and His throne must be there; how then can He be in the earth and can have an earthly throne? This is a difficulty with not a few; however, it is easily explained. Mount Zion in Jerusalem will be the place of the Lord's glory. That mountain will be lifted up in the coming age above all the other mountains, and on top of it there will rest the glory. This glory will be the glory of the New Jerusalem, which will extend upward into the heavens. It will be an unveiled glory, visible to the eyes of men. As we look now upon the starlit heavens and behold the countless stars, which declare the wisdom of God, so in the age to come the earth dwellers will look up and see in the air, in the heavens, a vision of undescribable beauty and glory, and then the heavens will declare the righteousness of Jehovah.

When Jacob went out from Beersheba and went

towards Haran he saw in that night in his dream
the heavens opened and a ladder was set upon the
earth and the top of it reached to the heavens. And
the angels of God ascended and descended upon
it; Jehovah stood above (Gen. 28). There can be
no question that our Lord had this heavenly vision
in view when He said: "Verily, verily, I say to
you, Henceforth ye shall see the heavens opened,
and the angels of God ascending and descending
upon the Son of Man" (John 1:51). Never has
this been fulfilled. The time for its fulfilment will
be when Jehovah-Jesus is King, and then there shall
be a wonderful intermingling of the heavenly and
the earthly, a glorious intercourse between the Jerusalem above and Jerusalem in the earth, and the
ladder, so to speak, will be Mount Zion.

The Lord, the King, will reign and manifest His
glory in Jerusalem; His glorious rest and throne
is over Jerusalem, in the heavenlies. In Jerusalem
will stand the throne of David, and it is the Lord's
throne, but there will also be a vice-regent of Christ
in the earth, a lineal descendant of David, who will
occupy the throne under Jehovah-Jesus. All this
will become clearer as we have Scripture after
Scripture relating to the kingdom pass before our
view.

In the book of Psalms, where we found such a
mine of prophetic teaching, we shall find much more
relating to the kingdom as promised to Israel and
as it shall be established by the return of the King,

our Lord. To quote all is again an impossibility. In the 2d Psalm we hear the Word of God when the tumult of the nations is at its height.

"And I have anointed my King upon Zion, the hill of my holiness. I will declare the decree; Jehovah hath said to me, Thou art my Son, this day have I begotten thee. Ask of me and I will give thee nations for an inheritance, and for thy possession the ends of the earth. Thou shalt break them with a sceptre of iron, as a potter's vessel thou shalt dash them to pieces" (Psalms 2:6-9).

The New Testament gives us a perfect commentary to these words. In Hebrews 1:5 we learn that it is the Lord Jesus Christ who is addressed as above, "Thou art my son," and in Acts 13:33 we read that it is His Sonship in resurrection which is declared. "God hath fulfilled the promise unto us, their children, in that He has raised up Jesus again"; as it is also written in the 2d Psalm, "Thou art my Son; this day have I begotten Thee." That He, as the Son of Man, is to be enthroned and receive the dominion of the earth, is here clearly indicated. The homage, the kissing of the Son, will take place when He has come; "Wherefore also God highly exalted Him, and granted Him a name, which is above every name; that at the name of Jesus every knee should bow, of heavenly and earthly and infernal beings, and every tongue confess that Jesus Christ is Lord to God, the Father's glory." (Phil. 2:9-11).

In the 8th Psalm the Son of Man, under whose

feet all things are put, who has the dominion of the earth, is our Lord (Heb. 2).

The 9th Psalm, which follows, contains the rule of Him who was made a little lower than the angels, and who is to rule as King in the earth.

"Jehovah sitteth forever; He has ordained His throne for judgment. And it is He that will judge the world in righteousness; He shall execute judgment upon the peoples with equity" (11:6, 7).

The 16th Psalm foretells clearly the resurrection of Him who became obedient, obedient unto death, and the 18th Psalm, as we learned before, shows the manifestation of the King, Jehovah. At the close of this Psalm praise is given for Jehovah's loving kindness, which He shows to the seed of David forever more. The King in the 21st Psalm is none other than the Son of Man, Jehovah-Jesus. His heart's desire is given to Him. He has a crown of pure gold and has length of days for ever and ever. Majesty and splendour is laid upon Him and He is made a blessing forever. All this could not mean David, but it means David's Son and David's Lord. The 22d Psalm, that Divine portrait of the suffering One, reveals not only death, but resurrection, life, and the kingdom as well.

"All the ends of the earth shall remember and turn unto Jehovah, and all the families of the nations shall worship thee. For the kingdom is Jehovah's, and He ruleth among the nations" (22:27, 28).

All this is often explained as meaning a spiritual rule. However, inasmuch as the sufferings of the Lord were literal, and the entire first part of the 22d Psalm was literally fulfilled, the second part will be likewise literally fulfilled. The kingdom will come, and *then*, and not before, the families of the nations will worship the King.

The 24th Psalm is another kingdom prophecy:

"Lift up your heads, ye gates, and be ye lifted up, ye everlasting doors; and the King of Glory shall come in. Who is this King of Glory? Jehovah strong and mighty, Jehovah mighty in battle" (24:7-10).

Then the earth will be Jehovah's, and the fulness thereof, the world and they that dwell therein. If we could follow Psalm after Psalm we would discover many precious revelations concerning the kingdom to come. The 45th Psalm reveals the King, who is fairer far than the sons of men, and who is addressed as God at the same time. He is seen coming with the sword girded at His side, and His enemies fall under Him; then it is said: "Thy Throne, O God (Christ—Hebrew 1:8), is for ever and ever; the sceptre of Thy Kingdom is for ever." The Psalms which follow show the kingdom established in the earth, with Jerusalem the city of a great King and Jehovah in possession of the earth.

"All ye peoples clap your hands; shout unto God with the voice of triumph! For Jehovah, the Most High, is terrible, a great King over all the earth" (Psalms 47:2).

"For God is the King over all the earth; sing psalms with understanding. God reigneth over the nations; God sitteth upon the throne of His holiness" (verses 7-8).

"Great is Jehovah, and greatly to be praised in the city of our God, in the hill of His holiness. Beautiful in elevation, the joy of the whole earth, is Mount Zion, on the sides of the north, the city of the great King" (48: 1, 2).

It is true these prophetic Psalms are mostly read now in Christian rituals or sung in a spiritualized form to elaborate music, and their great prophetic meaning is not recognized. The city of the great King mentioned above is Jerusalem, and Mount Zion will be elevated and becomes beautiful, the joy of the whole earth, because in the top of that mountain the heavenly Glory will rest. We shall see so later from the Word.

The 65th, 66th, 67th, and 68th Psalms are kingdom Psalms. Here again we find Zion the centre. It is the appointed place from which the rule and the blessing go forth.

The 68th Psalm is extremely rich. It is a wonderful prophetic picture of the future. The Psalm begins with that word which Moses spake by Divine command when the ark was moved:

"Let God arise, let His enemies be scattered, and let them that hate Him flee before Him. As smoke is driven, thou wilt drive them away; as wax melteth before the fire, the wicked shall perish at the presence of God." (Psalm 68: 1, 2).

As the Lord was then with this people, so will He be with them again and scatter the enemies. In the 16th and 17th verses we read also of the mountain of God.

"Why do ye look with envy, ye many peaked mountains, upon the mount that God hath desired for His abode? Yea, Jehovah will dwell there for ever. The chariots of God are twenty thousand, thousands upon thousands; the Lord is among them; 'tis a Sinai in holiness."

This is Zion, once more the seat of Jehovah's glorious government in the coming kingdom age. Who the King is who rules there is seen in the 18th verse of this Psalm: "Thou hast ascended on high, Thou hast led captivity captive." It is our Lord who descended and who ascended and led captivity captive. He came down and He went up again. And in the beginning of the kingdom, He comes down to establish His rule, and ascends, and again He descends in His glorious Person, as the King, and receives in the earth the homage of the nations. Of this more in our next chapter.

And what shall we say of the 72d Psalm? It is one of the most complete prophecies of the theocratic kingdom and its extension which it pleased the Holy Spirit to give. "For Solomon," reads the inspired heading of the Psalm, and Solomon means "Peace." Peace on earth when He comes and His kingdom rules. Righteousness and peace kiss each other. This Psalm reveals Him, the true and everlasting Melchizedek, King of Righteousness and King of Peace. His dominion will be from sea to sea, the dwellers of the

desert will bow before Him and His enemies lick
the dust. "Blessed be His glorious name for ever;
and let the whole earth be filled with His glory.
Amen and Amen. The prayers of David the son
of Jesse are ended." These are the words with
which the Psalm closes. How significant that at
the close of such a revelation of the kingdom,
David, to whom the revelation was made and who
is the instrument, says: "The prayers of David the
son of Jesse are ended"! He says with this: The
end has come; what Jehovah promised to me, David,
He has fulfilled; my prayers are ended, for they are
answered.

The 89th Psalm, which closes the third book
of the Psalms, brings once more the Davidic
covenant into the foreground and the kingdom
which will be established.

"I have made a covenant with mine elect,
I have sworn unto David my servant:
Thy seed will I establish for ever,
And build up Thy throne from generation to generation.
    Selah.
And the heavens shall celebrate thy wonders, O Jehovah,
And Thy faithfulness in the congregation of the saints."

(3-5.)

Here we have the earthly and heavenly glory
predicted. When the throne of David is established
and Jehovah rules, then will the heavens celebrate
the wonders of Jehovah; and they are wonders of
grace. "And the heavens shall declare His righteousness" (Ps. 50:6).

In the 89th Psalm we also read of the Son of David, the one who is the vice-regent of the King of kings, and who sits as prince upon the throne in Jerusalem. From verses 29-32 the prince of David and his earthly seed throughout the kingdom age is before us:

"And I will establish his seed for ever, and his throne as the days of heaven. If his sons forsake my law and walk not in mine ordinances; if they profane my statutes and keep not my commandments, then will I visit their transgressions with the rod, and their iniquity with stripes."

In the 96th to the 100th Psalm we have a series of prophecies which reveal the coming of Jehovah and His reign over the earth. He is come to judge the earth in righteousness. In the 97th Psalm we read once more that the heavens declare His righteousness, and all the peoples see His glory (verse 6). The heavens declare now the wisdom of God, the Creator, and His omnipotence. When the kingdom has come the heavens, besides declaring still God's wisdom, will declare the righteousness of Jehovah as in the heavenlies, the church, that one body with its millions and millions of glorified members, all sons with Him in glory, will be seen. They will look up and behold His glory, and we look down and see the earth subdued and ruled in righteousness.

That this Psalm and all its revelations is connected with the coming of the King is also proven from the New Testament. The Holy Spirit quotes the 7th verse in the 1st chapter of Hebrews, "Worship Him, ye angels." "And again when He brings in the firstborn into the habitable world, He says: Let all the angels worship Him" (Heb. 1:6). This should be a conclusive argument for any Christian believer, that Christ is coming to the earth again, that He will step into the habitable world worshipped by angels, and that the 97th Psalm is a kingdom Psalm, relating to the rule of Jehovah in the earth. Space does not permit to follow all this. The reader can search for himself and find Jehovah's place above the earth (verse 9), His worship as King (98:6), His reign and greatness in Zion (99:1, 2), and many other events in connection with the kingdom. But we have to pass by the many other Psalms and quote from only one more, the 132d.

We learn from the 1st verse that David and his endeavour is in view. Then in the 11th verse we read of Jehovah's covenant with David again:

"Jehovah hath sworn unto David,
  He will not turn from it:
  Of the fruit of thy body will I set upon thy throne.
  If thy children keep my covenant and my testimonies
      which I will teach them,
  Their children also shall sit upon thy throne.
  For Jehovah hath chosen Zion;
  He hath desired it for His dwelling;
  This is my rest for ever;
  Here will I dwell, for I have desired it."

From the great mass of passages found in the prophets which all relate to the theocratic kingdom we can call attention to but a few of the most striking, and to some others which will give additional light upon some of the statements made.

In Joel's ending vision of the day of Jehovah we read that "*then* Jehovah your God will dwell in Zion and Jerusalem shall be holy" (Joel 3:17). The book of Joel ends with the assurance, "Jehovah dwelleth in Zion," while the prophet Obadiah ends with that sublime word, "The kingdom shall be Jehovah's" (Obad. 21). In Amos we have the definite promise that in that day the Tabernacle of David, which is fallen down, will be raised up (Amos 9:11). This is the same of which Peter speaks, "The restoration of all things as spoken by the mouth of all His holy prophets," connected with the second coming of Christ (Acts 3:19). The throne of David will be raised up and become Jehovah's throne.

In Isaiah we find still more.

"And it shall come to pass in the end of days, that the mountain of Jehovah's house shall be established on the top of the mountains, and shall be lifted up above the hills; and all the nations shall flow into it. And many peoples shall go and say, Come, let us go up to the mountain of Jehovah, to the house of the God of Jacob; and He will teach us of His ways, and we will walk in His paths. For out of Zion shall go forth the law, and Jehovah's word from Jerusalem. And He shall judge among the nations and shall reprove many peoples; and they shall forge their swords into ploughshares, and their spears into pruning-knives; nation shall not lift up sword against nation, neither shall they learn war any more" (Isaiah 2:1-4).

THE THEOCRATIC KINGDOM

This is a picture of the theocratic kingdom and its earthly blessings. In the 4th chapter we read, in harmony with the testimony of the Psalms, that the glory of the Lord will dwell upon Zion (4:5). The 11th chapter in Isaiah manifests the King, the kingdom and the blessings with it. In the 25th chapter, verse 6, we hear that in *this* mountain Jehovah will make unto all peoples a feast of fat things, and in the 10th verse it is written, " For in this mountain shall the hand of Jehovah rest." Furthermore, the kingdom and reigning of the King is emphatically declared in the 32d chapter:

"Behold, a King shall reign in righteousness, and a Prince * shall rule in judgment, and a man shall be as a hiding place from the wind, and a covert from the storm; as brooks of water in a dry place, as the shadow of a great rock in a thirsty land" (verses 1, 2).

The 35th chapter shows the kingdom established. And how much else might be quoted from the second half of Isaiah—all the comforting promises of Jehovah being with His people and blessing them, the promises for the storm-tossed people and the downtrodden city, the desolate land—all will be fulfilled when the King reigns.

From Jeremiah we mention two passages which are so very clear and in fullest accord with all prophecies about the theocratic kingdom. In the 23d chapter we read:

* The prince is a son of David, the vice-regent.

179

"Behold the days come, saith Jehovah, when I will raise unto David a righteous Branch, who shall *reign as King* and act wisely, and shall execute judgment and righteousness in the land.

"In His day shall Judah be saved and Israel shall dwell in safety; and this is His name whereby He shall be called, 'Jehovah, our righteousness.'"

He is our Lord, the Branch, and as literally as He is *Jehovah Zidkenu,* so literally will He reign as King.

The second passage is still more significant.

"Behold, the days come, saith Jehovah, that I will perform the good word which I have spoken unto the house of Israel and unto the house of Judah. In *those* days and in that time, will I cause a Branch of Righteousness to grow up unto David; and He shall execute judgment and righteousness in the land. In those days shall Judah be saved and Jerusalem shall dwell in safety. And this is the name wherewith *she* shall be called: Jehovah our Righteousness. For thus saith Jehovah: There shall never fail to David a man to sit upon the throne of the house of Israel; neither shall there fail to the priests the Levites a man before me to offer up burnt offerings and to burn oblations, and to do sacrifice continually." (33: 14-18.)

Here Jerusalem is called " Jehovah our Righteousness," for she will be holy and the city of a great King. And once more the Word of Jehovah came to Jeremiah:

"Thus saith Jehovah: If ye can break my covenant in respect of the day, and my covenant in respect of the night, so that there should not be day and night in their season, *then* shall also my covenant be broken with David my servant that he should not have a son to reign upon his throne" (verses 20-21).

What a word this is! What a challenge of Jehovah! Oh, poor critics, blind leaders of the blind, what are you doing! You charge Jehovah with being untrue to His Word. But He challengeth, " Can you break the law of day and night? " If ye can, *then* my covenant with David will be broken. It is therefore *unbreakable.*

Ezekiel received likewise Jehovah's Word concerning the theocracy, and in this prophet we read much of the prince.

"And I will set up one shepherd over them, and He shall feed them and shall be their shepherd. And I Jehovah will be their God, and my servant David a prince in their midst; I Jehovah have spoken it" (Ez. 34:23, 24).

"And David my servant shall be King over them; and they shall have one shepherd; and they shall walk in my ordinances and keep my statutes and do them" (37:24).

From the 40th chapter on we have a prophetic description of the future temple for Jerusalem. In the 43d chapter we read that the gate towards the east is the place through which the glory of the God of Israel will enter in, and if we turn to the chapter which follows we find something else there.

"And he brought me back toward the outer gate of the sanctuary which looked toward the east; *and it was shut.* And Jehovah said unto me, This gate shall be shut; it shall not be opened, and no one shall enter in by it: for Jehovah, the God of Israel hath entered in by it; and it shall be shut. As for the *prince,* he the prince shall sit in it to eat bread *before* Jehovah: *he* shall enter by way of the porch of the gate, and shall go out by the way of the same" (44: 1-3).

After Jehovah, our Lord, has come and visibly shown Himself and passed through that gate it will be shut; only the *prince,* the vice-regent, has a place there. This prince cannot be our Lord, for he has a portion only of the land (45: 7).

Ezekiel closes with the change of name of the City of Jerusalem; her name will be " Jehovah Shammah "—the Lord is there.

The revelation of the kingdom in Daniel is so well known that we might pass over it. However, to make it complete, we speak of it briefly.

"And in the days of these kings shall the God of the heavens set up a kingdom which shall never be destroyed; and the sovereignty thereof shall not be left to another people: it shall break in pieces and consume all the kingdoms, but itself shall stand for ever. Forasmuch as thou sawest that a stone was cut out of the mountain without hands, and that it broke in pieces the iron, the brass, the clay, the silver and the gold,—the great God hath made known to the king what shall come to pass hereafter" (2: 44, 45).

This then is the first passage. Gentile dominion and world power, all forms of human government, monarchies and republics, will cease. A great catastrophe will fall upon Gentile rule. A stone out of Heaven falls down and strikes that image and it passes away, while the stone becomes a mountain filling the whole earth. The stone is Jehovah and His kingdom.

THE THEOCRATIC KINGDOM

"I saw in the night visions, and, behold, there came with the clouds of heaven one like a son of man, and he came up even to the Ancient of Days, and they brought Him near before Him. And there was given Him dominion and glory, and a *kingdom*, that all peoples, nations, and languages should serve Him; His dominion is an everlasting dominion, which shall not pass away, and His kingdom, which shall not be destroyed" (Daniel 7: 13, 14).

No need for further explanation of these verses. In Hosea the kingdom is likewise mentioned, for the children of Israel shall return and seek Jehovah, their God; and David, their King; and shall fear Jehovah and His goodness in the latter days (3:5).

The prophet Micah, who was contemporary with Isaiah, received the same vision which is contained in the 2d chapter of Isaiah (Micah 4: 1-4).

In Zephaniah we find a prophecy which confirms what we have learned so far.

"Jehovah hath taken away thy judgments, He hath cast out thine enemy. The King of Israel, Jehovah, is in the midst of thee; thou shalt not see evil any more" (Zeph. 3: 15).

In the prophet Zechariah we have numerous passages which predict the coming of the King and the world-wide kingdom, with its centre to be established in Jerusalem.

"Sing aloud and rejoice, daughter of Zion; for, behold, I come, and I will dwell in the midst of thee, saith Jehovah" (2: 10).

The crowning of the high priest Joshua with crowns of silver and gold was but a typical action.

It is a type of the crowning of Him who will be a priest upon His throne.

"Thus speaketh Jehovah of Hosts, saying, Behold, a man whose name is Branch, and he shall grow up in his own place and he shall build the temple of Jehovah; and he shall bear the glory, and shall sit and rule upon his throne, and the counsel of peace shall be between them both" (6: 12, 13).

In the 9th chapter a prophecy speaks of the King coming to Jerusalem. A part of it has been fulfilled, for the King was presented to Jerusalem, and if they had then received Him, all which the Spirit of God announces through Zechariah would have been soon fulfilled. But Jerusalem cast Him out, and the cry, "Hosanna, Son of David, King of Israel!" was changed to "Crucify Him! Crucify Him!" When He comes again the prophecy of Zechariah 9: 9-11 will come to pass.

"Rejoice greatly, daughter of Zion; shout, daughter of Jerusalem! Behold, thy King cometh to thee; He is just, having salvation; lowly and riding upon an ass, even upon a colt the foal of an ass. And I will cut off the chariot from Ephraim, and the horse from Jerusalem. And He shall speak peace to the nations; and His dominion shall be from sea to sea, and from the river to the ends of the earth."

Here we have once more the King, who is Jehovah, and His kingdom, world-wide to the ends of the earth, in perfect agreement with other prophecies.

In the last chapter of Zechariah that kingdom to come, Jerusalem its centre, and the nations gathering to Jerusalem, is most fully revealed. As we have seen before from this chapter, Jehovah comes to Jerusalem and His feet stand in that day upon the Mount of Olives. Then we read: "And Jehovah shall be King over all the earth; in that day shall there be one Jehovah and His name one" (verse 9). Zechariah likewise sees Jerusalem, and with it Zion lifted up. "And Jerusalem shall be lifted up and shall dwell in her own place" (verse 10).

Here is another kingdom prophecy:

"And it shall come to pass, that all that are left of the nations which came against Jerusalem shall go up from year to year to worship the King, Jehovah of Hosts, and to celebrate the feast of tabernacles" (verse 16).

But this will be sufficient after pointing out the most prominent passages which foretell the kingdom, which is to be established, to prove the perfect harmony of the entire prophetic Word on this topic, a harmony as Divine and complete as the other great events of the closing of this age and the beginning of the new.

"Wilt thou, Lord, at this time restore again the kingdom of Israel?" thus they had asked, as we mentioned in the beginning of this chapter. What perfect right they had to ask this question with such prophecies given through the mouth of God's prophets! The Lord Himself had taught them to pray in the prayer He gave to them, "Thy kingdom come," and it could mean only one kingdom, that kingdom which prophet after prophet describes and which is so prominent in the Psalms. It has been postponed, but it will surely come. It will come with the appearing of the King. It will come not gradually in a spiritual way, but it will come accompanied by tremendous upheavals, the tribulation, the day of Jehovah, the visible and glorious return of the Lord. What a foolish dream it is to claim a kingdom without the King; it is unscriptural. Well said old Dr. Chalmers, " You may talk as you please, but the Scriptures make it clear that this dispensation is going to end with a smash."

As believers we wait not for this kingdom nor for the King, but we wait for the Lord, our glorified head. Our prayer is not " Thy kingdom come," but " Even so come Lord Jesus." The dying thief cried out, " Remember me, Lord, when thou comest in Thy kingdom," but the Lord had something better for him, saved by grace, and told him, " Verily, I say to thee, *To-day* shalt thou be with me in Paradise."

Our portion is with the Lord in glory in the rule over the earth. He has made us a kingdom, priests to His God and Father. The kingdom in the earth has for its subjects Israel and the nations, but in the church, His body, it shall be fulfilled what is written, " That He might display in the coming ages the surpassing riches of His grace in kindness toward us in Christ Jesus." (Eph. 2:7).

IX

THE BLESSINGS OF THE COMING AGE— PEACE ON EARTH—GLORY TO GOD IN THE HIGHEST—ISRAEL'S SU- PREMACY AND MINISTRY — ALL CREATION BLESSED

LIKE one who ascends a high mountain, and the nearer he comes to the summit the grander becomes the view, so have we reached the consummation, and as we advanced the horizon has widened and the things to come were viewed by us. Now as we reach the summit and look out over the revelations of the prophetic Word and behold some of the bless- ings which are promised for the coming age, the age of the kingdom, the millennium, we shall have the grandest view of all. Many nations have rec- ords of a so-called golden age, which is to come, and their poets have written about it. But only in the Word of God have we a true description of that age and the blessings it will bring. Christendom generally believes in such an age of blessing, but it has, with its spiritualizing method, turned every- thing upside down. The millennium is generally put down as " the universal triumph of the church and the conversion of the world by the church."

Such a millennium as it is taught now was unknown in the apostolic age and for many centuries after. The present-day teaching of a Christless and king-less millennium originated in the beginning of the eighteenth century. Its father was a man who held wicked doctrine. Whitby, the originator of post-millennialism, the theory of a church-millennium without Christ having returned, denied the absolute Deity of our Lord and the Deity of the Holy Spirit.

Now the fact is, when the millennium comes it will not be an age of blessing *for the church* in the earth, for the church is then passed out of the world and rules and reigns with Christ, her Lord, in the heavenlies. The church has no promise of a millennium, but the blessings of the coming age are for Israel, the nations and creation.

And how rich and full is the revelation of this age of blessing, which will be ushered in with the mighty shaking of the heavens and the earth and the manifestation of Jehovah! We gave only a small portion of Scriptures in our preceding chapters describing these great coming events and showing the harmony of the prophetic Word; we shall be obliged to confine ourselves again to a few passages in treating this theme. By far the greater part of prophecies are prophecies of blessing in the coming age.

How numerous are the Scriptures which declare the blessedness of converted and restored Israel! His people, no longer the tail of the nations, but the Head and Jehovah's witness in the earth. Converted, born again, Spirit-filled, this nation will be at last God's "first born Son" in the earth, and bring nations to the new birth, so that converted nations, a thing *unknown* in this age, will be added unto Israel, the leader and head of the nations. Idolatry will cease completely. Blessings immeasurable will be upon Israel. They will walk now in the statutes of the Lord and keep His laws. Once more will the Word of Jehovah and the law go forth from Jerusalem and Zion, and nations will be taught to walk in these ordinances. Jerusalem will be the great centre of the world. There, as we saw before, the mountain of Jehovah's Rest, Zion, will be seen in all its beauty, and a most blessed intercourse between the heavens and the earth will take place, and the glory of Jehovah which appears there will spread like a canopy over the land; the knowledge of that glory will cover the earth as the waters cover the sea.

In Jerusalem there will stand a marvellous temple, which will be a house of prayer for all nations, and there an elaborate ritual will be kept. Nations and representatives of nations will come up to keep the feast of tabernacles. War will be unknown in the earth, for the Prince of Peace will speak to the nations and they will learn war no more; praise and worship will be in the earth. All creation will be blessed likewise. Groaning creation will be delivered and restored to its normal condition. But we have to quote some of these prophecies to learn of these blessings to come and see once more the perfect harmony of prophecy.

We turn again to the great prophecies which were before us throughout this volume. Balaam speaks through the Spirit of this age of blessing for Israel.

> " How goodly are thy tents, Jacob,
> And thy tabernacles, Israel!
> Like valleys are they spread forth,
> Like gardens by the river side,
> Like aloe-trees, which Jehovah has planted,
> Like cedars beside the waters.
> Water shall flow out of his buckets
> And his seed shall be in great waters."
>
> (Numbers 24: 5-7.)

Here we have a picture of Israel's blessedness, planted and kept by Jehovah. " The water flowing out of his buckets," is a prophecy which relates to the day when the living waters shall flow forth from Jerusalem; when the Spirit will be poured forth upon all.

The last verse of Moses' Song, which showed us so much, is a short and concise description of the coming millennium, and to this little verse prophecies recur again and again.

If we found so much in the Book of Psalms before, we shall find much more now. The descriptions of the blest and delivered nation, their joy and worship, the subdued earth, the joy of the nations, and other blessed events falling into the coming age are very numerous. In the 46th Psalm we read, " There is a river the streams whereof make glad the city of God, the sanctuary of the habitations of the Most High. God is in the midst of her; she shall not be moved. God shall help her at the dawn of the morning " (verse 4, 5). This will be when the new age begins and the river of God will flow forth from Jerusalem. The " eternal city," not Rome, but Jerusalem, will receive her help, her glory and exaltation at the dawn of the morning, when the Sun of Righteousness rises. In the same Psalm we read of another scene which will be at the beginning of the millennium.

" Come behold the works of Jehovah, what desolation He has made in the earth, He hath made war to cease unto the end of the earth; He breaketh the bow, and cutteth the spear asunder; He burneth the chariot in the fire " (verses 8, 9).

The two Psalms which follow contain millennial descriptions.

We take another illustration from the 66th Psalm:

" Shout aloud unto God all the earth; sing forth the glory of His name, make His praise glorious; say unto God, How terrible are Thy works! because of the greatness of Thy strength, thine enemies come cringing unto Thee; all the earth shall worship Thee, and sing Psalms unto Thee; they shall sing forth Thy name " (verses 1-4).

This description is followed by Israel's confession and calling upon the people to bless their God (verse 8), and their own worship, " I will go into thy house with burnt offerings; I will perform my vows to thee " (verse 13).

Much could be quoted from the 68th Psalm, but we call attention only to a few verses at the end.

"Because of thy temple at Jerusalem shall kings bring presents unto Thee. . . . Great ones shall come out of Egypt; Ethiopia shall quickly stretch out her hands unto God—Ye kingdoms of the earth, sing unto God; sing Psalms of Jehovah " (verses 29, 31, 32).

All this will be fulfilled when Jehovah has come and His glory is known in the earth, and because of that glorious temple in Jerusalem the kings come to bring their presents.

The kingdom Psalm, the 72d, gives the millennial blessings still more fully. Justice will be given then to the afflicted, the righteous will flourish, and there will be abundance of peace. " The kings of Tarshish and of the isles shall render presents; the kings of Sheba and Seba shall offer tribute; yea, all the kings shall bow down before Him; all nations shall serve Him " (verses 10, 11). " There shall be abundance of corn in the earth, upon the top of the mountains; the fruit thereof shall shake like Lebanon; and they of the city shall bloom like the herb of the earth " (verse 16).

Then famines will have an end and poverty will be unknown in that coming kingdom age.

The 84th and 85th Psalms are further prophecies of the blessings to come.

The BLESSINGS *of the* COMING AGE

"Thou *hast* been favourable, Jehovah, to thy land (Immanuel's land—Palestine); thou hast turned the captivity of Jacob. Thou *hast* forgiven the iniquity of thy people; thou *hast* covered all their sins" (85:1, 2).

We have seen before when this takes place. Not before the Redeemer comes to Zion and turns away ungodliness will the people Israel have forgiveness of sins. If we turn to the end of this Psalm we find what is revealed in connection with this event.

"Loving kindness and truth are met together; righteousness and peace have kissed each other; truth shall spring out of the earth, and righteousness shall look down from the heavens. Jehovah will also give what is good, and our land shall yield its increase. Righteousness shall go before Him, and He shall set His footsteps on the way" (verses 10-13).

This is the perfection and glory of the age to come. In the 96th Psalm and those connected with it we have a still wider description of the kingdom blessings.

"Worship Jehovah in holy splendour, tremble before Him, all the earth. Say among the nations, Jehovah reigneth! Yea, the earth is established, it shall not be moved; He will execute judgments upon the people with equity. Let the heavens rejoice and let the earth be glad; let the sea roar and the fulness thereof. Let the field exult and all that is therein. *Then* shall all the trees of the forest sing for joy" (verses 9-11).

The 103d Psalm is one which is used much in Christian ritual and song. Prophetically it is Israel's song throughout the millennium, and other nations will learn to sing that song after Israel.

"Bless Jehovah, O my soul; and all that is within me bless His holy name. Bless Jehovah, O my soul, and forget not all His benefits; who forgiveth all thine iniquities and healeth all thy diseases. Who redeemeth thy life from the pit, who covereth thee with loving kindness and tender mercies" (verses 1-4).

A similar song of praise is the 113th Psalm. It will be sung in the millennium, and Jehovah's name will be praised from the rising of the sun unto the going down of the same. The Psalm closes with that significant verse:

"He maketh the barren woman to keep house as a joyful mother of sons. Hallelujah."

The barren woman who will be a mother is Israel.

The shortest of all the Psalms, the 117th, refers us to the coming age, while the longest Psalm, the 119th, gives the description of the righteous nation occupied with the law and the Word. How Jehovah will keep His people in the age to come is learned from the 121st Psalm. The 122d Psalm is a beautiful one. It shows how they go up with rejoicing into the house of Jehovah. They go there in the millennium to give thanks unto the name of Jehovah. "For there are set thrones for judgment, the thrones of the house of David." Peace, too, will be in Jerusalem. This shows the time when this will be. But we dare not tarry longer in these precious songs in which the Holy Spirit reveals the high and blessed position of redeemed Israel in th' earth, in the midst of the nations. As we read through the fifth book of the Psalms we find that praise to Jehovah increases and there is not a word said that it will ever stop. Israel praises Jehovah, the nations praise Him, and all creation, mountains and hills, beasts and all cattle, creeping things and flying fowls, every thing that hath breath, will praise Jehovah.

Our view into these coming earthly glories widens as we turn to the prophets. That judgment and restoration chapter, Joel 3, gives us a glimpse of the millennial glory.

"And it shall come to pass in *that day,* that the mountains shall drop down new wine, and the hills shall flow with milk, and all the watercourses of Judah shall flow with waters; and a fountain shall come forth from the house of Jehovah, and shall water the valley of Shittim" (verse 18).

We must leave it to the reader to find the perfect agreement of all these prophecies relating to the blessings of the coming age and to find them is an easy task, with the key we have given.

In the 2d chapter of Hosea we find a predictive description of the blessings which Jehovah will give when He has arisen and had mercy upon Zion.

"And I will make a covenant for them in that day with the beasts of the field and with the fowls of the heavens, and the creeping things of the ground; and I will break bow and sword and battle out of the land; and I will make them to lie down safely. And I will betroth thee unto me for ever; and I will betroth thee unto me in right-

195

eousness and in judgment and in loving kindness and in mercies; and I will betroth thee unto me in faithfulness; and thou shalt know Jehovah. And it shall come to pass in that day, I will hear, saith Jehovah, I will hear the heavens, and they shall hear the earth; and the earth shall hear the corn, and the new wine, and the oil, and they shall hear Jezreel" (2: 18-22).

And in the last chapter of the same book of Hosea we read the assurance that Israel shall then blossom as the lily and his beauty shall be as the olive tree.

Richer than all other prophets is Isaiah in his God-given visions of what is in store for Israel, the nations, and the entire creation. Such perfect blessings for this sin-cursed world are unfolded here that the searcher becomes overwhelmed by the wonderful and gracious ways of our God and Father, and praises Him that He has made known these exceeding great and precious things. We quoted from the 2d chapter before without looking at the details of the Word which Isaiah *saw*. Here, as well as in Micah 4, we read the nations shall come to Jerusalem, to the house of Jehovah, to be taught by Him, and that the nations will learn war no more and lift no longer a sword against other nations. Now a universal peace is attempted by an international court of arbitration, and it—fails. Peace on earth will only be when the Prince of Peace comes and begins His rule over the nations.

Turning to the 11th chapter we find still more here. Groaning creation is delivered from the curse

196

resting upon it now and restored to its normal
Edenic condition.   There is no warrant whatever to
spiritualize these familiar words, " The wolf also
shall dwell with the lamb, and the leopard shall lie
down with the kid, and the calf and the young lion
and the fatted beast together," etc. (11:6-10).
These words mean what they say.   When the first
Adam with his helpmeet stood in the garden all
creation was subjected to them; neither did the leopard spring upon the kid to tear it to pieces.   Sin,
coming in, changed all.   But now the last Adam, the
second man, has everything put under His feet (in
this age we see *not yet* all things put under Him—
Heb. 2).   With Him in that age to come is His
bride, the church, and His earthly bride, Israel.
Then that deliverance for which all creation waits
will have come.   Other millennial events in chapter
11 we are obliged to pass by.   The 12th chapter
is redeemed Israel's song of praise, so harmonious
with many of the Psalms.

The 25th chapter may serve to put another millennial scene before us.

"And He will destroy in this mountain (Zion) the face
of the veil which veileth all the peoples, and the covering
that is spread over all the nations.   He will swallow up
death in victory.   And the Lord Jehovah will wipe away
tears from off all faces; and the reproach of His people
will He take away from off all the earth: for Jehovah hath
spoken" (25:7, 8).

In the 26th chapter Israel's glad millennial praise

is once more recorded, and in the 35th chapter we find additional promises to be fulfilled in the kingdom age. The wilderness will be glad and the desert will rejoice; "they shall see the glory of Jehovah, the excellency of our God" (verse 5).

"Then the eyes of the blind shall be opened, and the ears of the deaf be unstopped; then shall the lame man leap as the hart, and the tongue of the dumb sing; for in the wilderness shall waters break out and torrents in the desert. . . . And the ransomed of Jehovah shall return and come to Zion with singing; and everlasting joy shall be upon their heads; they shall obtain gladness and joy, and sorrow and sighing shall flee away."

What an age it will be when all this has come literally true!

With the 40th chapter we find many more prophecies relating to the topic of our chapter.

"Behold I do a new thing; now it shall spring forth; shall ye not know it? I will even make a way in the wilderness, and rivers in the waste. The beast in the field shall glorify me, and the jackals and the ostriches; for I will give waters in the wilderness, to give drink to My people, My chosen. This people have I formed for Myself; they shall show forth My praise" (43: 19-21; see also 41: 18-19).

Here is Jehovah's address to the nations, and His chosen people Israel will deliver the message to them:

"Gather yourselves and come; draw near together, ye that are escaped of the nations. They have no knowledge that carry the wood of their graven image, and pray unto a god that cannot save. Declare and bring them near; yea, let them take counsel together: who hath caused this to be heard from ancient time? Who hath declared this long ago? Is it not I, Jehovah? And there is no God else besides Me; a just God and a Saviour, there is none besides Me. Look unto Me and be ye saved, all the ends of the earth; for I am God and there is none besides else. I have sworn by Myself, the word is gone out of My mouth in righteousness and shall not return, that unto me every knee shall bow, every tongue shall swear. Only in Jehovah shall one say, have I righteousness and strength" (45: 20-24).

From the 49th chapter we select another passage:

"Behold, these shall come from afar; and behold, these from the north and from the west and these from the land of Sinim. Shout, ye heavens; and be joyful, thou earth, and break forth into singing, ye mountains; for Jehovah hath comforted His people, and will have mercy upon His afflicted ones" (verses 12-13).

The 53d chapter makes known the suffering Servant of Jehovah, that is the Messiah, Jehovah Himself, and His atonement as well as Israel's confession that they knew Him not. Upon this confession and the assurance of the exaltation of Him who went into death, follows a chapter which falls entirely into the coming age. Read through this chapter and learn still more of Israel's Hope and its full realization after this present age is passed. It is precious to read all this now.

"Thou afflicted, tossed with tempest, not comforted! Behold, I will set thy stones in antimony, and lay thy foundations with sapphires, and I will make thy walls with rubies and thy gates of carbuncles and all thy borders of precious stones. And all thy children shall be taught of Jehovah and great shall be the peace of thy children" (54: 11-13).

And in the 55th chapter it is written:

"For ye shall go out with joy, and be led forth with peace; the mountains and the hills shall break forth before you into singing, and all the trees of the field shall clap their hands. Instead of the thorn there shall come up the cypress, and instead of the nettle there shall come up the myrtle; and it shall be Jehovah for a name, for an everlasting sign that shall not be cut off" (verses 12, 13).

Still more impressive become these predictions of blessings to come, as we turn to the end of this prophet.

There are three chapters so full of millennial prophecies, the 60th, 61st, and 62d.

In the 60th, Israel is told that nations shall walk by her light. She is to lift up her eyes and see the multitudes from the nations and from the sea coming unto her. In the 6th verse we read: "They shall bring gold and incense, and they shall publish the praises of Jehovah." It is generally said this was fulfilled in the wise men coming to Bethlehem to worship the young child. However, the wise men brought gold, incense, *and myrrh.* Myrrh typifies the bitterness of death. Those coming in the millennium, according to the verse above, bring no myrrh, because the sufferings are now passed.

Again, that coming glorious age is described in the following words:

"For bronze I will bring gold, and for iron I will bring silver, and for wood I will bring bronze, and for stones iron; and I will make thine officers peace and thy rulers righteousness. Violence shall no more be heard in thy land, wasting nor destruction within thy borders, but thou shalt call thy walls salvation and thy gates praise. The sun shall be no more thy light by day, neither for brightness shall the moon give light unto thee, but Jehovah shall be thine everlasting light and thy God thy Glory. Thy sun shall no more go down, neither shall the moon withdraw itself; for Jehovah shall be thine everlasting light and the days of thy mourning shall be ended" (60: 19, 20).

No more sun then for Jerusalem, because a brighter Sun, the Sun of Righteousness, the Glory of Jehovah, shines above Jerusalem.

In the 61st chapter Israel is seen as the priest among the nations, ministers of God they are called, and the chapter ends with Israel's hymn of praise (verse 10) and a short description of the blessings among the nations.

"For as the earth bringeth forth her bud, and as a garden causeth the things that are sown in it to spring forth, so the Lord Jehovah will cause righteousness to spring forth before all nations" (11).

Just as rich is the 62d chapter, and at the close of the 65th chapter the Spirit of God speaks even more fully of what Jehovah, the Jehovah who was made sin for us, who was raised from the dead and returns in power and glory, will do. We must quote this:

"But be glad and rejoice for ever in that which I create. For behold, I create Jerusalem a rejoicing and her people a joy. And I will rejoice over Jerusalem, and will joy in my people; and the voice of weeping shall no more be heard in her, nor the voice of crying. There shall be no more thenceforth an infant of days, nor an old man that has not completed his days; for the youth shall die a hundred years old, and a sinner being a hundred years old shall be accursed; and they shall build houses, and inhabit them; and they shall plant vineyards, and eat the fruit thereof: they shall not build, and another inhabit; they shall not plant, and another eat; for as the days of a tree shall be the days of my people, and mine elect shall long enjoy the work of their hands, they shall not labour in vain, nor bring forth terror; for they are the seed of the blessed of Jehovah, and their offspring with them.

" And it shall come to pass, that before they call, I shall answer; I will hear.

" The wolf and the lamb shall feed together, and the lion shall eat straw like an ox; and dust shall be the serpent's meat. They shall not hurt or destroy in all my holy mountain, saith Jehovah" (verses 18-25).

It would take many pages to expound this most interesting prophecy. We take it literal; why should we not? When it says " dust shall be the serpent's meat," it means most likely that of all animals only the serpent, the instrument of Satan once, will still have the mark of the curse " crawling upon its belly " during the millennium. The last chapter of Isaiah adds still more to these complete visions of the blessings in the coming age. Here again we read, " And it shall come to pass from new moon to new moon, and from Sabbath to Sabbath, all flesh shall come to worship before me, saith Jehovah." And outside of Jerusalem there will still be seen the carcasses of the men which sinned against Jehovah, and in that mass the worm is not dying and the fire is not quenched (24th verse). It is a most solemn warning, for glorious as that coming age is it ends too with man's failure. Satan, bound a thousand years to seduce the nations no more, becomes loosed for a little while and finds in his final revolt abundant material among the nations.

From Jeremiah we take but one passage, which perhaps is less familiar to readers of prophecy. It is in chapter 16: 19-21. The verses before tell us of Israel being brought back from the nations, their coming great restoration. In connection with this we read the following:

"Jehovah, my strength and my fortress in the day of distress (thus will Israel say), unto Thee shall the nations come from the ends of the earth, and they shall say, Surely our fathers have inherited falsehoods and vanity; and in these things there is no profit. Shall a man make gods unto himself and they are no gods? Therefore, behold, I will this once cause them to know my hand and my might; and they shall know that my name is Jehovah."

This tells us that idolatry will cease on the earth. Ezekiel's wonderful description of the millennial temple and its ceremonies we cannot follow now. Suffice it to say that such a glorious temple, a house of prayer for all nations, and Levites attending to the ceremonies, will be built in the coming age. What a house it will be!

Of the many, many other passages which might be quoted we give but a few from the prophet Zechariah.

"And many nations shall join themselves to Jehovah in that day, and shall be unto me for a people" (2: 11).

This word stands in the night vision in which the prophet sees the restoration of Jerusalem and the return of Israel to their land. It is, therefore, that day in which nations shall join themselves to Jehovah.

The 8th chapter in Zechariah is another chapter which treats of the restoration and the blessings in connection with it.

"Thy seed shall be prosperous, the vine shall give its fruit, and the ground shall give its produce, and the heavens shall give their dew; and I will cause the remnant of this people to possess all things" (verse 11).

"Thus saith Jehovah of hosts: Yet again shall there come peoples and the inhabitants of many cities; and the inhabitants of one city shall go to another, saying, Let us go speedily, to supplicate Jehovah and to seek Jehovah of hosts; I will go also. And many peoples and strong nations shall come to seek Jehovah of hosts in Jerusalem and to supplicate Jehovah. Thus saith Jehovah of hosts: In those days shalt ten men take hold, out of all languages of the nations, shall even take hold of the skirt of him that is a Jew, saying, We will go with you; for we have heard that God is with you" (verses 20-23).

It was promised to Abraham that through his seed all the nations of the earth are to be blest. Here is the fulfilment. Israel's land, the centre of the world. Jehovah's glory spread over it will be the goal of the desires of the nations of the earth during the millennium. Then as the Jew goes among the nations and shows himself there, the nations will no longer cast him out and ridicule him, but they cling to his skirt and ask him to take them along to the glorious land.—Through Israel world conversion at last. In the 9th chapter of Zechariah we read once more of " Peace on Earth," for " He shall speak peace to the nations."

In the last chapter of Zechariah the nations are also seen coming to Jerusalem to worship Jehovah, and that Jerusalem will be a holy city. Malachi, who describes the Return of Jehovah as the rising of the Sun, says it will be with healing beneath His wings. Healing for Israel, for the nations and for groaning creation.

But is there anything said in the New Testament? We read little of it there. This has led some to say that the blessings spoken of in the Old Testament Scriptures must mean the church. The reason why the Epistles say nothing on the millennium is because the millennium is not for the church. The church is like the sheet which Peter saw. It came out of heaven and it was taken back again. The church belongs to the heavenlies, and she is not to be blessed with the earthly things and expect a fulfilment of earthly blessings.

Nevertheless, do we find a witness of the Holy Spirit in the New Testament. Our Lord preached not only the kingdom of the heavens to be at hand, but with His preaching came the signs of that kingdom. The multitudes were miraculously fed, the blind saw, the deaf heard, and the lame leaped (Isaiah 35). In the 19th chapter of Matthew He speaks as sitting upon His own throne in the *regeneration.* By regeneration He means the coming age. Still clearer does that age stand out in the great chapter of our redemption in Christ, Romans 8. There the Spirit of God speaks expressly of the deliverance of groaning creation, and that term includes all, Israel, the nations, and the rest of creation. The deliverance will take place when the sons of God will be manifested. The sons of God will be manifested when He, the first-born, comes forth from glory. In the book of Acts we read also of it, when it is said that after the Lord has returned and the tabernacle of David is built again the residue of men will seek the Lord. (Acts 15.) From the book of Revelation we learn that this coming age will last a thousand years; for this reason it is called a millennium. (Rev. 20: 1-6.)

God has revealed His plans, and He wants us, the future heirs of all things with His Son, to know *now* a little of the things to come. Oh, why are we so slow to take hold of them? How different it would be with all of us if we would search, and search deeper and deeper, in the Word of our God and let the Spirit of God show us these things to come!

CONCLUSIONS

WE have briefly shown in this volume the harmony of the entire prophetic Word concerning the great future events to come. It would have been an easy task to enlarge each chapter and add hundreds of passages from the Word of God. What we have written and give in this volume, however, seems to us sufficient to prove conclusively two great and important facts. The first fact proven is the wonderful harmony of the prophetic Word, and the second fact, springing from the first, is the verbal inspiration of the Old Testament Scriptures. No sane man would believe that such a perfect agreement in the description of these coming events, written by so many different men, living centuries apart, writing independently of each other, is of purely human origin. That these men wrote down their own imaginations, their own thoughts, and that the Spirit of God had nothing to do with it, is harder to believe than the fact which we have demonstrated, that this wonderful harmony is supernatural.

Our aim has likewise been to produce a short handbook of Old Testament prophecy, and point the way to a better and more correct understanding of the little read and less studied prophetic books.

If under the blessing of our Lord some of His children receive help through this volume, and our little work will be used to open up God's precious Word to some hearts and unfold some of God's gracious purposes, we shall thank and praise Him for it in all eternity.

May the blessing of our Lord rest upon every reader, and, living in these significant times, when the fulfilment of all this volume teaches is so near, may we all be " like men who wait for their Lord."

FINIS

Index to Scripture Texts

INDEX

INDEX

211